HOME EC
for the
DOMESTICALLY
CHALLENGED

S0-BMW-788

HOME EC
for the
DOMESTICALLY CHALLENGED

BY

PETER WRIGHT
author of
Cook Like a Mother! Clean Like a Pro!

2004 TORONTO, CANADA

Ordering information:

Distributed in Canada by Hushion House Publishing Ltd.

36 Northline Road Toronto, Ontario Canada M4B 3E2

Phone (416) 285-6100, Fax (416) 285-1777

National Library of Canada Cataloguing in Publication

Wright, Peter, 1956-

   Home ec for the domestically challenged / Peter Wright.

Includes index.

ISBN 0-9689462-1-6

1. Cookery. I. Title.

TX355.W75 2004   641.5'12 ·   C2004-901075-1

Cover / book design: Karen Petherick,
                            Intuitive Design International Ltd., Markham, Ontario
Illustrations: Michael Petherick and Colleen Lynch
Cover Photo: Helen Tansey Photography

Printed and bound in Canada

Disclaimer: Although recipes have been tested, the author does not assume any responsibility for errors.

This book is dedicated to

the two most cherished people in my life:

Spencer and Taylor

CONTENTS

PREFACE

Not Knowing is Not Funny

I have a confession to make. I'm not a cooking and cleaning keener. In fact, I all but detest cleaning and I certainly don't stay up late conjuring up miracle meals. As a college student and bachelor, cooking was a necessity. As a single father, cooking became a challenge because I was determined to become good at it out of a desire to feed my kids the kind of meals I grew up with. However, like many who decide to become better at something, I didn't know what I didn't know. I thought my cooking skills were pretty good. I could make a great wok meal – really two meals, one with chicken and vegetables and the other with beef and vegetables – and the same thing for pasta. Whenever I tried to prepare a new meal with a recipe someone gave me, however, I'd get frustrated because terms were used that I didn't know and assumptions were made that baffled me. I didn't know how to add "divided" spices; I didn't know the difference between sautéing and braising; and I didn't know the bathroom implications of cross-contamination.

Cleaning was a whole other story. Cleaning made me feel like Superman – holding Kryptonite. Ever had the feeling that you're going to die if you spend any more time at a task? Why is it we find cleaning so unappealing? Two reasons come to mind. One, time: everyone's busy; we all have things we need to do for school, our careers, our fitness, our fun. On the list of priorities, cleaning is pretty close to the bottom. Two, knowledge: it's hard to find satisfaction in a task if you don't know how to do it and you don't have the best possible tools to do it well and quickly – tools you probably don't have because you've been buying the cheapest and crappiest stuff you can find.

So, armed with an apparent paradox – a fierce determination to feed my kids and myself and keep the house functionally clean, while not really wanting to learn how – I researched everything. I researched food safety practices. I researched the best time to add spices. I researched nutrition labels. I researched the impact of different fats on our health. I researched cooking terms. I even researched what material makes the best pots. And so on and so on.

I wrote this book to provide like-minded cooking and cleaning non-keeners with a practical way to do the things they don't necessarily like or know how to do, and do them better. If you've joined that club, it will help you make choices based on fact and practicality rather than the desire to emulate a Home Ec keener. I tried to find a balance between how those Moms of a few generations ago made things happen and how we can get things done, given today's career, financial and family realities. My aim with this book was to examine what those Moms knew and see what version of it we could create. Call it Home Ec Version 2.0. And don't worry; it's not about how to be creative with household items and make a floor wax from the casings of old shotgun shells and papaya.

What it all boils down to, I believe, is finding your place in this land of cooking and cleaning, a land that without question you will visit again and again for the rest of your life. It's your call whether you grind your teeth every time you visit, or do as I have done, and learn how with technology, a little know-how and a light-hearted attitude, you can get things done so effectively it'll make you laugh, or at least smile.

INTRODUCTION

Great Mix:
Advertising *and* Apathy

Home Economics
"The science and art of home management."

The American Heritage® Dictionary of the English Language

The science and art of home management. Home management. Sounds funny, doesn't it? Sounds as anachronistic as wringer washers and iceboxes. It conjures up images of Mom in a black and white photo, smiling in front of an open oven, holding a freshly baked pie with one hand and vacuuming with the other, while keeping an eye on dinner.

Mom knew everything about homemaking back then. She knew the science behind a great meal; she knew nutrition and how to plan our meals; she knew how to mend our clothes, what materials were best for what purposes, what foods to shop for, how to get the best deals, and so on. Mom knew all these things because she was supposed to. There wasn't a cooking question Mom couldn't answer. But in this day and age, proficiency in Home Ec has fallen into almost complete obsolescence – partly because people are just too busy and because they don't realize how important it is.

Is being too busy to learn the basics taking a toll? Is it just a coincidence that the number of food-borne illnesses, usually from improper food handling, is astronomical? The Centers For Disease Control estimates that 76 million people get sick, more than 300,000 are hospitalized, and 5,000 Americans die EACH YEAR from food-borne illness. Is it also just a coincidence that the rate of obesity is growing so fast it's beyond tragedy? No.

In fairness, though, Home Ec takes time, something we don't have. It requires knowledge to make informed decisions, something we're apathetic about learning. And the millions and millions of advertising dollars being spent every hour to convince us to eat things that no one in their right mind would eat on a regular basis appear to be winning the nutrition battle. Fast food is like the entertainment industry version of eating: you have to suspend your disbelief when you eat it. You have to convince yourself that the grams of fat, salt and sugar you're eating will somehow slide from your arteries like oil in a non-stick pan. It seems that Advertising and Apathy combine to make a mighty, potentially impenetrable, foe.

So, the question has to be why do we continue to eat this way and what can be done to curb the growth of kidney disease, diabetes and obesity? It's not my intention to go on about how our careers and responsibilities make it difficult to properly take care of ourselves, or how it takes a Herculean effort to resist the daily onslaught of commercials that badger us to eat their sugar and salt and chemical-laden goodies.

Instead, I want this Home Ec lesson to be governed by a famous "Decree" that, loosely paraphrased, tells of having the patience to put up with things we can't change, the courage to change what can be changed, and the brain cells to know which is which. This applies to many things, of course, but especially to us because there are some domestic rules that can be broken and some that have to be adhered to, and the challenge for the beginner is knowing which is which.

1

Stuff to Make It With: Stock Up!

Home Economists (i.e., professional Moms) are judged by the kind of meal they can assemble from scratch, meaning, the things they already have in the kitchen. They have contests to see what gourmet meal they can produce using only the stuff on the bottom shelf in their pantry. They are the kitchen's equivalent to TV's *Survivor*. How does that relate to the rest of us? Well, our mission is to copy the pros to the outer limits of our personalities. It's pretty plain to see that how we stock our cupboards, our fridge, our freezer and pantries will have a direct impact on how evolved we can become as a Home Engineer.

This chapter is geared towards helping you develop your own well-stocked, flexible and ultimately very useful kitchen.

Stuff to Make It With

I think one of the biggest challenges a new cook faces is knowing what to buy at the grocery store, a place they don't get to very often. Should they buy canned tuna or salmon, chicken or ham? What's the best deal? What offers the greatest number of meal possibilities? For that matter, what's the best kind of tuna – not make, but kind – as in, flaked or chunk, light or white? Professional Moms would know this.

The second thing a professional Mom seems to know is what you can skimp on and what you can't. This chapter will show in detail the stuff you should have around the house, as well as an insight into what is interchangeable and what's NOT interchangeable.

The following is a list of stuff that you can accumulate over time, or in one fell swoop. This list has been chosen not just to reflect personal preferences but because of the meal possibilities that exist.

Freezer

Frozen vegetables	buy the name brand broccoli flowers or California vegetables
Ice cream	buy anything but the cheapest
Frozen lasagna	anything but the individual-size ones
Frozen shepherd's pie	for those brain-dead times
Sandwich bags of lean ground beef	buy the bulk thing of lean ground beef, divide into usable portions, and chuck into the freezer for times when you're in a wicked hurry

Fridge

Don't forget, we're after options here.

Having the following things in your fridge at most times opens up tasty, fast, healthy OPTIONS.

Pillsbury Crescent Rolls	this is a comfort option
Broccoli	these are healthy options
Carrots	
Celery	
Peppers (green, red)	
Cheese	
Yogurt	
Hot dogs	speedy, tasty options
Ketchup	
Mustard	

Spice Cupboard

We tend to take spices for granted because so many meals come prepared and pre-spiced, but there's a good reason our ancestors were willing to weather water and wind just to find the Orient and its cache of spices. When you can turn an adequately cooked meal into something people want more of and talk about for ages, you've turned the corner from domestic dork to domestic don.

Olive oil (extra virgin is considered the finest)	this will be for the recipes where you're paying a lot of attention to taste
Safflower, canola oil	these oils are considered healthy choices because they derive a high percentage of their total fats from *mono- and polyunsaturated* fats. They also have high smoking points, good for general frying.
Salt/pepper	if you can afford it, one of those salt/pepper combo things is great – if you like coarsely ground salt and pepper. The free-flowing stuff is best for cooking, but for eating, the coarsely ground stuff is a nice change.
Oregano	
Basil	
Thyme	
Spice Hunter roasted garlic	this is so good you'll want to sprinkle it on your cereal
Garlic salt	if you can't find the above
Coarse pepper (ground)	for cooking
Seasoning salt	
Lemon pepper	this is a super spice for fish
Soya sauce	when you go wokking!
Steak/chicken BBQ seasoning	
Balsamic vinegar	this seems to be the vinegar of choice for most recipes and the choice of women who want to contribute to dinner by making a salad
Powdered stocks	if you have some Knorr vegetable, chicken or beef powdered stock, you're in for a taste upgrade

Food Cupboard

I know buying all this stuff seems like a pain, so try to do occasional big grocery-shopping expeditions rather than many little ones. Or, if your city has one of those on-line grocery services, try it. The one I use charges about $6 for delivery and a minimum order of $60, but it's such a treat having someone else schlep your groceries to the door.

Kraft Macaroni and Cheese	yes, there are times you legitimately can resort to Kraft Macaroni and Cheese (KD)
Pillsbury One-Step cookies/brownies	
Crackers (saltine)	
Pretzels	these are so low in fat they're worth getting used to
Chocolate syrup	
SNACKS	for me, the challenge of snacks is, if they're readily available they're already in my mouth. So, do like Mom did: you can have X amount per week. Period. If you eat them all the first day, that's your (and your colon's) problem.
Instant (Minute) rice	all right, from a healthy perspective, this is not a Grade A choice. Think of it as a dinner equivalent to sugar cereals: they've had nutrients added that give some semblance of nutritional value, but in essence, both are similar to eating fortified sawdust. Buy the brown rice that is more finicky and takes more time if you're concerned about health.
Pasta sauces	I've a confession to make: there's no question the prepared sauces offer a more "complex" taste, but if you have the time, it's healthier to make your own.

Diced tomatoes	Why? Because you can make more things with diced tomatoes than you can with whole ones that you'll end up mushing anyway.
Pasta, different shapes*	(rigatoni, penne, bowtie, spaghetti)
Tuna	flaked or chunk white. Flaked is my preference because it already comes whacked up – no one likes a big honking piece of tuna. The light may be cheaper – for a reason: it's the hotdog of the tuna world.
Hamburger Helper	if you keep it at the back of the cupboard so no one knows there are days your meal-planning brain stalls
Lipton side dishes	if you remember the sort of meals we grew up with – meat and scalloped potatoes, or a pork chop and smashed potatoes, these are what Lipton gives us with their SideKicks. They're awesome because they're the closest to achieving an authentic Mom-made taste and are incredibly easy to make.
Flavored rices	these are great too and can be made in a terrific hurry
Potatoes	sometimes the low-tech things get mentioned last
Cereal (kind of obvious, I know)	I buy a sweetened (Apple Cinnamon Cheerios), a mid-range, semi-healthy cereal (Just Right), and a senior's cereal (All-Bran). I could argue I buy all these as a choice for kids, adults and seniors, in that order, but the truth is I do a triple-decker every morning.

Canned soups for cooking	Consommé (or Beef Broth), Cream of Broccoli, Cream of Chicken, Cream of Mushroom, Cream of Asparagus. Domestic newcomers have a tough time believing they'll ever use these types of soups, but one day, sometime soon, you'll be pouring a can of Cream of Asparagus soup over something.
Lipton Soupworks	these are arguably better than canned soups, closer to homemade. And if you really want them to take a homemade "step up," add frozen vegetables to them.
2 lb bag of onions	if you're not a big cook, a 2 lb bag is the way to go. But try to always have a bag on hand, because of how onion fills out the taste of most ad-libbed recipes.

You may have noticed there's no mention of potato chips. That's because I really like them and the only way I'm not going to eat them is if I don't buy them. Also, crackers are a good, lower-fat substitute everyone manages to get used to. For a treat, say, the Super Bowl, I'll buy chips.

* The reason for having so many different pastas is simple: some days you need a change of pace, and different pasta, as unimpressive as it sounds, can do the trick.

Liquor Cabinet

It took me a long time to figure out the advantages of having liquor in the house that wasn't necessarily intended for me. I may not like Scotch, but having it on hand in case the boss shows up, pays dividends. Buy these as the budget allows:

Scotch	your boss probably doesn't drink Bud
Bailey's Irish Cream	nor does his significant other
Cognac	in case some card game starts up
Good dry white wine	in case the bridge club stops by
Grand Marnier	and stays
Your choice of beer	you drink it, no one else can
Not your choice of beer	you won't drink it; everyone else can

Lastly, it's important for you to know how to use existing information. By this I mean asking the right people. I know this could be a direction-asking reluctance thing, but get over it – I ask everybody questions. I ask the butcher to suggest cuts of meat for the meal I'm preparing and I ask how to cook certain meats. Aside from raising my cooking confidence, asking questions of these people seems to make them feel good, too. Ask the ones who look as though they may have at one point in their lives made dinner.

2

Stuff to Make It In: What Does What

This chapter could just as well be called "Stuff Your Mom Used That's Been Improved so Your Time in the Kitchen Goes By Faster and Better," but I felt that title lacked a little oomph. I find, in all honesty, it's tough to know what does what – let alone well – if you haven't been taught. It's tough to know how much something has improved if you haven't been frustrated by how things were in the first place. It's even tougher to know what works and what doesn't if you don't really care, and that's how I'm hoping this book will be of value to you.

Why? Because I didn't care about this stuff either – until I was responsible for making meals day in, day out. I can assure you there will come a time when you will value this information. As someone who has tried to make decent meals in the absence of readily available items that can make a terrific contribution to my efforts, I've had to stumble up a steep learning curve to discover everything can be so much quicker – in all senses of the word, from cooking to clean-up – when you use the right device.

How you fare as a cook and cleaner in your house largely depends on your choice and deployment of tools.

The following are devices I want you to get – it doesn't matter whether you ask for them for Christmas, birthdays, whatever.

- Auto turn-off coffee maker
- Can opener
- Casserole dish
- Containers for leftovers
- Cookie tray

- Cookware
- Cutting board
- Indoor grill
- Kitchen gadgets
- Knife set
- Measuring cup (glass)
- Meat thermometer
- Microwave oven
- Oven mitts
- Roasting pan
- Rotisserie oven
- Timer
- Toaster oven
- Utensils
- Wok

Device Details and Deployment

Any Make of Auto Shut-Off Coffee Maker

I know this is a small point, but sometimes you have to have things that think for themselves.

Can Opener

Opening a can used to be a source of confusion for me when it came to the lid. There seemed to be only two options: one involved the lid falling into virginal food – the lid of a can that's had more handlers than Michael Jackson – and the other option turned your can into a counter-mounted guillotine. The second option was okay if I was alone in the kitchen, but if my kids were around, reaching into the cupboard for a glass, it was a source of concern. I'm pleased to report that I've found a can opener that's made by Starfrit, called the Securi Max, that effectively addresses both concerns by turning the lid into something that just pops off without any sharp edges on either the lid or the can – like the end of a can of frozen orange juice. The added benefit is if you live in an area that has recycling and you need more real estate in the blue box, you can just whip off both ends and flatten the can – again, without creating a medieval break-out-of-jail device.

Casserole Dish

Seriously. Having a decent casserole dish means you can make tuna casserole or some sort of hamburger rice dish that doesn't have a name.

Containers for Leftovers

I'm a big fan of leftovers – knowing there's something good in the fridge that means I don't have to make dinner still makes me weep with gratitude. However, one of the biggest tragedies that can befall a leftover lover is when something you're coveting makes an unscheduled – and quite unceremonious – visit to the floor, providing a living example of the expression, "add insult to injury." Not only do you have to clean up the mess, but you don't get to enjoy your anticipated goodies. Which containers don't deal well with being accidentally knocked out of the fridge or falling to the floor on their way from the fridge to the counter? Well, margarine containers for sure, and any of the "disposable" food storage containers, such as Ziploc or TakeAlongs. The line I've found that can withstand the occasion drop (even from the roof, should I happen to be up there) is the Starfrit Lock and Lock line of food storage products. The television commercial for them has the product in the dishwasher during a cycle, and then the homeowner takes it out and eats the contents (which I think was meant to demonstrate its air-and water-tight properties). They have a 4-way locking system so you can be confident whatever goes in stays in until you decide it's time – an asset when you're taking stews and soups for lunch.

Cookie Tray

Nothing can double as a cookie tray, so don't bother looking. And the uses for cookie trays go beyond the fairly obvious: they can also be used under anything that might spill into your oven. Spilling in your oven means an eventual cleaning, so try your best to avoid this. Also, buy a good cookie tray, one with a non-stick surface. Why? Goes back to the less-time-in-cleaning-up drill.

Cookware

There's no question this section could be the focus of a **series** of books, not just one section in *a* book, so I'll have to give you the *Reader's Digest* view of what things are, what they do and which ones I like for the reasons I like them.

In a way, choice of cookware has its own hierarchy: if you're a pro, you use copper or stainless steel; if you're a traditionalist, you use cast iron; an everyday cook or beginner probably uses non-stick; and if you like shiny, low-care, you'll choose stainless steel. There are two key issues we need to address around cookware:

1.   Products and use
2.   Materials and benefits

Here's a list of some of the most important things you'll see as you stroll through the kitchenware department at Sears:

Fry pans	these are products you'll use almost every time you cook, unless you're cooking a casserole. Use them for sautéing, frying, browning, braising and so on.
Saucepan	use this with a steamer for your vegetables, or to cook/warm up sauce or soup.
Dutch oven /stock pot	Dutch ovens are like saucepans except they have two handles instead of one long one. They're used for soups, chili.
Steamer	some pots will have a specially designed insert.
insert	Although these fit better than a standard steamer, unless you get the entire package as a gift, they're not worth it.
Lids	this seems like an afterthought, but consider the lids that come with the cookware: they will either be your best friend (i.e., do what you ask and make your life easier) or they'll be one of those friends that always seems to let you down.

Everything has its pros and cons, so here's what's up:

Materials   Pros/Cons

Copper	PROS	• conducts heat evenly and is very responsive, making it one of the best choices for frying and sautéing • heats and cools quickly
	CONS	• extremely expensive • minor things: it can have chemical reactions with almost everything – even moisture in the air can cause a film to form that (yikes!) is poisonous. Also, salty foods can have a metallic taste. • needs to be polished regularly
Stainless steel	PROS	• keeps bright shine and has good strength • does not corrode • moderately priced
	CONS	• does not conduct heat well • not the easiest to clean if you were called away at an inopportune time and left things on the element.
Cast iron	PROS	• great to recreate the meals our Moms made, as they give a special texture and taste almost impossible to achieve with either stainless steel or non-stick
	CONS	• upkeep is prohibitive – needs "curing" periodically, is predisposed to rusting if not properly stored
Non-stick	PROS	• reduces the amount of fat required to cook • very forgiving from both a cooking and cleaning perspective (you have to go out of your way to burn something and extremely out of your way to require scrubbing)
	CONS	• pans are manufactured by a process that "punches" a flat piece of material into the shape, requiring a piece thin enough to be "punched." The manufacturers recommend we don't use high heat or metal utensils because the non-

stick film will be "compromised." Compromised, in this case, is another word for "have to buy a new one." Case in point: I had one that I babied and used only during demonstrations; I only used medium heat, and was very careful with it. The surface looked new – as it should have, being only six months old. Problem was, it was becoming a concave fry pan (bottom was arching inwards). It was like cooking on a ball.

Aluminum	PROS	• inexpensive • responsive and good conductor of heat • does not distort when heat is cranked • is present as a heat conductor in the bases of most cookware, even stainless steel, because of heat distribution qualities
	CONS	• can react to certain acidic foods, causing corrosion that can affect the taste of the food
Anodized aluminum	PROS	• good conductor of heat • special finish offers good non-stick properties
	CONS	should be washed by hand, not dishwasher

All cooks, especially entry and mid-level ones, are looking for the perfect marriage between aesthetics, performance and clean-up. The ideal blend of materials would combine the results of cast iron (predictable heat, great texture and taste, ability to use metal utensils) with the modern convenience of non-stick – in an attractive set. After my experience with the concave pan, I began looking for the perfect fry pan that would marry all these features.

My search revealed there's a whole new material that does indeed have the multi-feature marriage certificate:

Cast aluminum with a titanium-based non-stick coating, found in the **Starfrit** and **Heritage** line of cookware. The cast aluminum provides superior heat distribution with absolutely no warping, buckling or bending even when forgotten on the stove on high heat (hey, I don't have TiVo, so if it's a late, 4th quarter drive, some things get overlooked). The coating is reinforced with titanium, a material developed by NASA to protect the space shuttle from the heat of the sun, as it absorbs excess heat. This material called "Quantanium," (they probably developed this titanium product while on a Qantas flight) is much stronger than the steel of metal utensils, thus protecting the pans from their owners' daily use ... or abuse.

These products offer something you don't see very often: a guarantee against warping, something we non-stick fry pan users would love to have had many years – and pans – ago. But, in all fairness, it's not just the material that gives them the confidence to offer a guarantee: it's the manufacturing and design. The pans have a base that's 7mm thick, compared to my old nonstick pan that was probably less than 3mm. Remember how most non-stick pans were made, using the "punch-out" system? These babies start life as a molten concoction and are poured into a mold, a method that allows for varying thickness of product. This allows for areas that are deemed more structurally important, such as the base, to be thicker and stronger than one lousy piece of sheet metal whacked into a uni-thick shape. This is all very technical, I admit, but knowing it may save you time, aggravation and ultimately money while looking for products that let you cook like Mom without a great deal of skill.

One last thing, though (I love new stuff!): the manufacturers of the Starfrit and Heritage lines of cookware say their product is "scratch resistant." They have to say "resistant" in the same way watches are water "resistant" to 300 meters: 99.9 times out of 100 they work. Under usual cooking conditions (making a meal after work, trying to make something the kids will like that's healthy), this Quantanium non-stick surface repelled my advances with a knife to cut through a piece of chicken, as well as my using a metal utensil with considerable vigor. What benefits does it provide the everyday cook? Two, really:

1. You don't have to worry about cranking up the heat to get

things going as fast as possible – something my other non-stick pans warned against – so you don't have to pussyfoot around your cookware; and

2. You don't have to worry about doing what's necessary to get the meal on the table so you can get the hell out the door – like having to baby the pan when cutting a piece of meat in it to see if it's done.

Cutting Board

It's tricky to be cutting stuff on plates or on counter tops. The plates may be clean, but frozen chicken breasts or pork chops can get a little skittish on them. And using countertops, aside from their state of hygiene, isn't a good choice either (knife marks are frowned upon by landlords and real estate agents). No, the best way is to use a cutting board. Look for ones that offer an antibacterial component and have some sort of run-off trough. Recent research has suggested that wooden cutting boards may be better than plastic from a bacteria-elimination perspective. Some experts feel that wood absorbs and eliminates bacteria better when it's cut into, whereas plastic and other materials, for the most part, can preserve bacteria for weeks.

Indoor Grill

For anybody who lives in a climate-challenged area, these things are a must. Anything that gives me options not requiring a parka or an umbrella has my vote.

Kitchen Gadgets

It's always been a source of amusement to me that there are so many products out there that can make our lives easier if we'd just keep a look-out for them. For a lot of people, domestic stuff has the same effect on them as a strong anesthetic. They're too numb to realize there are some very effective domestic tools, and by not paying attention to what's new, they're forced to keep using things that are archaic and inefficient. It's tricky to know what works and what's best left in the store. I'm going to give you an idea of the kitchen tasks that can be made easier with the right tools:

Cutting	for a detailed look into knife options, see the chapter Stuff You Should Know
Peeling	buy one like the Chef'n'Popout Peeler

Washing	get one of those lettuce washers. Why? They're fast
Steaming	buy a vegetable steamer – even a metal one (as opposed to electric)
Straining	for pasta to vegetables to draining fat from cooked ground beef, you will need one
Meat thermometer	a meat thermometer is to the novice cook what the "undo" command is to a computer neo-nerd. It means you never have to worry about unwittingly harming yourself or your children by under-cooking something. Forget "wait until the juices turn from pink to clear" for chicken or turkey. Forget wondering exactly how many pounds the thing was. Just jab it with your trusty meat thermometer. Of course, this assumes you're following some sort of cooking time per weight equation. But more about that later.
Timer	If we're after Mom-like meals, we're after meals that have good taste and texture, two things that are the by-product of good timing, something that's completely out of reach for a novice cook without a timer. DON'T assume you'll remember when to turn things or retrieve them from whatever hot spot you left them in. Having to remember to check the clock, etc., adds the one thing we're working hard to avoid: tension.
Knife Set	(See Stuff You Should Know for a complete breakdown of knives, but for now all you really have to know is to get as good a knife set as you can afford.) One of the greatest pleasures a man can have (in the dining room) is being the carver for Thanksgiving or Christmas dinner. As the gleaming knife slices through the turkey you cooked to perfection, your girlfriend, kids, parents, cousins, stragglers and so on, look at you lovingly and anticipate their dinner. As you pass them plate after plate of finely sliced meat, they marvel at your skill as a carver and as a cook. All is right in the world with a sharp carving knife. Of course, a different scenario takes place if you don't have a sharp knife:

you have the pleasure of shredding off pieces of meat so small they're perfect for the turkey casserole or sandwiches to follow.

The best thing to do is either request a knife set for a gift or go to a store that has knowledgeable staff and ask them to recommend a versatile knife set for the kind of stuff you'll be doing. Don't buy the cheapest set. There's a reason they're cheap: the metal doesn't hold an edge or can't achieve an edge. I have one of those sets that comes in a wooden block. I like it because it's handy and you don't have to root through your drawers with greasy hands looking for the right knife. A good set should include a bread knife, a couple of paring knives, a honking cleaver for those reluctant chicken parts (I have to admit, I don't use the cleaver very often but once in a while it's great to come crashing down on a piece of meat), and a couple of full-bladed knives.

Manual Food Processor	Food processors are great, but kind of a pain to drag out, plug in, use, and clean, plus they are generally expensive. I prefer the manual ones because they're easy to use and clean. The only manual one I know of is the Starfrit Manual Food Processor.
Measuring Cups	These are essential, even with my casual approach to measuring ingredients. Get the glass ones because the plastic ones feel and look cheap, if for no other reason.
Microwave Oven	I only use one for thawing meat or warming up coffee. Researchers feel even steaming vegetables in them shortchanges the nutrients you end up with, so use a microwave oven judiciously.
Oven Mitts	Having burnt myself too many times using hand towels to retrieve cookies or something from the oven, I'm now a card-carrying spokesperson for the Oven Mitt Society. And having burnt myself too many times with run-of-the mill oven mitts, I'm now a big believer in those blue silicone babies that protect you up to temperatures beyond what your oven can

generate (575 degrees F!). Get them if you like protection.

Roasting Pan	How the hell do you propose cooking like Mom if you don't have a simple roasting pan with cover that costs maybe $10? Seriously, buy a bigger one than you think you need. Ask the sales people (one that looks like she's turned on an oven at some point in her life) to recommend one that could do up to a 20 lb turkey.
Rotisserie Oven	Have you seen the infomercials for Showtime Rotisserie Ovens? Well, in my never-ending quest for really tasty meals made really easily and quickly, I got one. It's unbelievable. The ability to season, pierce and place a chicken on the rotisserie, slide it in place, put the timer on, and put some vegetables for steaming on the top gives this appliance top marks in our Make it Quick, Make it Tasty school of cooking. You save a trip to the store every time you want the delicious flavor – and aroma – of rotisserie cooking (I know it's kind of obvious, but this sort of thing still amazes me).
Toaster Oven	For anyone with limited kitchen counter real estate, these are a must. Toaster ovens can double for your big oven. These babies can bake cookies and poach a salmon. They can also make toast, which I know comes as a surprise to many.
Utensils	A good set of utensils should include: a large, firm plastic ladling spoon (you don't want a spoon that becomes wimpy as you're stirring steaming sauces or soups), a straining spoon the same size, and a spatula. You can have wooden spoons if you wish, but don't get cheap ones that melt if you leave them in whatever you're making. I've got some utensils that have metal handles with a blue silicone working end. Why would you want these? Because, like the oven mitts, they have a higher than average heat resistance, so you could even leave them on a BBQ grill and they wouldn't melt (not something you want to do, but you know what I mean).
Wok	You know why woks are the perfect cooking tool for

guys? Clean up. All you need is one of those little whisk things you get when you buy your wok. Put the wok under running water, use the whisk to get rid of whatever you cooked, and dry. No detergent required. You can use either a non-stick version or an authentic Chinese wok, doesn't matter. From an ease-of-use perspective, I have to tell you one thing. For the longest time, I was a proponent of an authentic Chinese wok. I put up with the challenges they posed (they come with a ring that sits over the element and focuses the heat to the base of the wok, but that also, by accident, makes the wok tilt all over the place so you end up jamming the handle into your chest to keep it level), because I thought that was part of the experience. Recently I tried a non-stick cast-aluminum version that sits directly on the element. The cast aluminum let me achieve and maintain a high cooking heat without having to wrestle a handle, and obviously clean up was just as easy. So, it's your call.

Stuff Mom Knew: Home Ec Defined

In the old days, if Home Ec had been a computer, my guess is Mom would have been the software, Dad, the hardware. Mom had the answer to any question involving what went on your back to what went in your mouth. If you had a question about your physical world, as in why the front wheel on your bike kept flying off when you did a wheelie, Dad had the answer. Dad had the answer because his dad had the answer. How did Mom know all these things? Well, in those days she wouldn't have been considered much of a Mom if she didn't know how to make dinner for the family – much in the same way Dad wouldn't have been considered much of a Dad if he couldn't fix the kitchen cupboard door that Mom kept banging her head on. But Mom not only knew what her mother knew, she also attended classes in school to hone her domestic skills. What exactly is a domestic skill?

Mom knew:
- How to make a tasty dinner from scratch
- How to set a budget (before the days of overdraft protection)
- How to prepare a shopping list
- How to food shop (how to make sure you got only what you came for)
- Cooking times (how to prepare a meal so everything's cooked and ready at once)
- Meal selection (as in, how to avoid bologna stew 7 days in a row)
- How to read recipes
- How to make good meals, day in, day out
- Food handling
- Cooking methods

Mom did:

- The food shopping
- The best she could with the budget she had
- All she could to ensure we were eating healthily
- The laundry
- The housework
- The social skills teaching
- The manners teaching
- The shopping list preparation, and used coupons and sales to stretch the food budget

In our age of prosperity, however, we've grown to feel we don't have to budget or make a list, we can forego sales and we can just choose food based on what we feel like rather than be influenced by what we need to stay healthy. An informal study of this could involve going to a grocery store in an affluent area and one in a rent-control area, and seeing which location has the greater number of shoppers using a list. A lot of people are embarrassed about looking for specials, to say nothing of walking around carrying a list: lists are for old ladies wearing those rain bonnets that fold into a little packet, not us. We're smart people, and smart people don't forget why they went to the store! That's why we're making more trips to the grocery store than ever before.

But Home Ec for the Domestically Challenged is a book about how we can achieve the benefits of traditional home economics at a time when no one has the time, interest, or knowledge, for that matter. So, before we can create a modern version, we need to understand what Moms of a certain generation knew and how they got things done. So, back to ol' Mom.

What did Mom do back then?

Ironing

Ever see the irons they had back in the day when Mom did Dad's shirts and pants? No wonder she looked haggard – ironing with those things was probably like dragging lawn furniture sideways across a cornfield.

Cleaning

In the early days of the "we-must-have-a-clean-house" mentality, it required deep sacrifice and an entire day to get the house clean – especially since the cleaning products back then lacked the technology to power up on the cleaning quotient. So, rags, buckets, hot water, powdered cleanser, 60 lb vacuum cleaners and stepladders were the order of the day. It was also quite a workout, which is probably why one rarely saw excessively overweight women 40 years ago – today, only elite triathletes could endure a day of house-cleaning with those tools.

Pie-making

This is something that only dedicated cooks and grandmothers are any good at now. Back then, ol' Mom could make a cherry pie that would make you swear allegiance to the National Order of Valiant Drivers, if that's what she wanted.

Dinner-making

There seemed to be a never-ending source of meal ideas – I should say, dinner, because lunch was kind of the same thing all the time. Mom was able to make dinner at the drop of a hat, and of course it always included the major food groups, and rarely involved anything packaged.

Budget

The ol' man and her set a budget to spend on groceries. It could be argued things were a lot easier then, meaning, people didn't have the same concerns about what they were eating – everything was good for you as far as they were concerned. Nobody was concerned about trans fatty acids or polyunsaturates or mono sodium glutamate. They were mainly concerned with how much it cost.

However, it's no argument to say that the budget was the budget: there was no overdraft protection, no buying of groceries with a credit card, and certainly, no savings accounts to speak of. So, when Mom had $50 for groceries, that's what she had. If she was able to buy it all for $40 and buy herself a bottle of wine, that's known as a *domestic engineer's pecuniary incentive.*

List

Lists are goofy things, for sure; they can indeed make you look like a ninny. It's a fact. When I'm storming around the grocery store buying stuff for my Cooking for the Domestically Challenged class, I'm very purposeful, as I walk the aisles with my list. I can't afford to rely on my memory in these cases; if I forgot something, my credibility would be compromised. But that doesn't really matter. What matters is that even when I'm professionally forced to use a list, I have tinges of weenieism. Most of us are so concerned with how we look ("Are you looking at me? Are you looking at me?"), we prefer to forget things and return umpteen times than carry a list. Mom would have carried a list, for sure.

Food shopping

Moms of that era were nothing if not extremely disciplined. They were highly trained sales-hounds, and anything that got in their way didn't stand a chance. Shopping with a Mom of that generation was like accompanying a Brigadier General surveying the troops – they knew what they were looking for and you'd better keep up and shut up for the entire tour – or else.

Cooking times	Can you remember many meals growing up when dinner was funky, as in, gross? No. It may have been gross sometimes because dinner wasn't to your liking, but it wasn't because it was undercooked. Why? Because Mom knew the cooking temperatures and times for various meats. Mom was also a master at making sure dinner was ready at once, regardless of how many elements she decided to include.
Meal selection	Moms of that era knew they were single-handedly responsible for ensuring their families were well fed, which, for them, meant nutritionally well-fed, not just a pantry full of Doritos. Mom seemed to have a notion of what meals to make according to season, as well as how to rotate meals to avoid the "oh-my-god-are-we-having-that-again!" syndrome.
Recipe reading	Mom knew how to read a recipe, otherwise how would you expect any one human being to remember how to make 400 dinner ideas? But the key to what Mom knew was what component of the recipe could be altered to tailor and improve it, and what components of the recipe had to stay put.
Good meals	Day in, day out. Within budget. There's no question, a lot of meals we had depended on what was on Sale. If you go into a store with an aunt or some other relative from my mother's generation, you'll see them scouring the aisles for sales. Something the average domestically challenged person doesn't realize is that grocery stores reward people who are paying attention. I'll admit it takes an evolved domestic engineer to buy pork chops ONLY because they're on sale, not because they represent tonight's dinner. Remember those beans and hotdogs you had

called "Lumberjack Stew?" You can bet hotdogs and beans were on sale those weeks. Remember scalloped potatoes and sausages? Yep, I'll bet sausages were on sale.

Food handling | Fifty years ago there weren't many cases of food poisoning – or they just didn't know enough to recognize it. But, for the most part, Moms knew basic food handling principles: they knew to wash their hands before cooking, and so on (there's an extensive section on proper food handling methods in the next chapter).

Cooking methods | Most Moms knew that it wasn't enough to be able to make tasty meals; they had to be able to use different cooking methods to give their tasty meals a completely new texture.

But how did Mom know these things? Was she born with this knowledge? I'm going to stand still so she can kick me in the arse for even jokingly suggesting this. No, to give you a clear idea of where this stuff came from, here's an example of a Home Economics Curriculum high schools had in 1937:

Part I. – Health and Nutrition

Specific Aims.

1. To develop an appreciation of the advisability of careful planning of meals to meet the needs of the various members of the family and yet conserve time, energy, and money.
2. To develop an understanding of the relation of food to health and a keen and intelligent interest in maintaining sensible food habits.
3. To develop the ability to plan balanced meals for a family on a low-level income so that the highest nutritive value may be obtained for the money expended.
4. To develop an understanding of the importance of receiving health information from reliable sources.

Hmmmn. So they got taught these things.

Part II. – Foods and Cookery
Specific Aims.
1. To develop the ability to secure greater satisfaction from money spent for food in a home.
2. To develop a desire to assume greater responsibility for the planning, preparing, and serving of attractive meals in the home in varying circumstances.
3. To develop skill in cookery commensurate with the time apportioned to practical work.
4. To develop an appreciation of the principles underlying the best methods of cooking various types of food.

Part III. – Social Customs and Courtesies

Part IV. – The Dining Room
Note. – It is advisable to study this unit concurrently with Meal Service.

Part V. – Laundering
4. To develop an appreciation of the advancement in improvements in modern laundry equipment.

But I think my favorite is:

Part XII
Specific Aims.
1. To develop an appreciation of the advantages of a pleasing personality in home, social and community life.
2. To develop a realization of the importance of family life and a desire to help create a happy home.
3. To develop some understanding of the management problems of the home and a willingness to share responsibility for activities carried on in the home.
4. To develop an understanding of how location, size, arrangement, and equipment of the home affect home life.
5. To give information and to develop judgments that will enable girls to spend more wisely that part of the family income for which they are directly concerned.

6. To create a desire to acquire the desirable characteristics of a good citizen and to help in developing a more satisfactory community.

(Another hhhmmmn. There are a couple of points here that are sorely needed in today's curriculum. I'm sorry; did I say that out loud?) Don't you love reading that stuff?

This gives us a clear picture of why things got done the way they got done. It also tells us a lot about how dedicated Moms were in taking care of us. So, now the trick is to find out how we can take this info and create a modern blueprint of Home Ec.

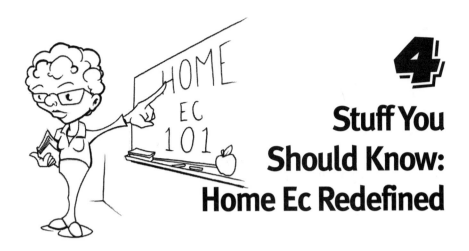

4

Stuff You Should Know: Home Ec Redefined

A woman I play tennis with is a Registered Dietician, with an Honors Bachelor of Science in Home Economics. She studied food science as it relates to nutrition, which I'm mentioning because there are many educational pursuits available to people with a genuine interest in the role nutrition plays in people's lives. My aim, on the other hand, is to provide timely information that could eliminate some of the decision-making concerns new cooks face when standing slack-jawed in the kitchen, wondering what to do next. It's the sort of information that comes in real handy, like when you're replacing a screw on your bike brakes and it's taking a long time: is it taking so long because it's a very long screw with a fine thread that should take a long time to screw back in – or has it taken so long because you are indeed stripping the thread, something you won't know until you're gliding down a steep hill and go to use your brakes? The difference is important. Same thing with **Stuff You Should Know**: one misstep with food preparation is the difference between a weekend with your pals and a weekend with the toilet.

Just to put some relevance to our ruminations, The Centers for Disease Control and Prevention (CDC) estimate that simply washing hands and improving food-handling practices could prevent 97% of food-borne illnesses. So, if you want to avoid the 24-hour flu season all year long, follow these rules (there's no such thing, by the way, as a 24-hour flu: it's a mild or severe case of food poisoning. Reminds me of the time I bought some of that bruschetta topping from a local grocery store and spent the night marveling at how many orifices could eject parsley ... but, anyway ...).

Food and Kitchen Safety

Before we start to cook any meals, though, we need to be aware of the most common kitchen mistakes that can lead to food poisoning:

- Unclean hands
- Counter-top thawing
- Leftovers left on the counter for more than 2 hours before refrigerating
- Unclean cutting board
- Same spoon to stir and taste
- Marinating at room temperature
- Marinating with contaminated marinade (what the meat has been lying in)
- Too much time between fridges (store and home)
- Raw and cooked meats on the same platter
- Shared knife for raw meat and vegetables
- Leaving canned food in the can and refrigerating

There are some fundamental things that entry-level cooks should know and I'm going to try to deal with the most obvious.

Unclean hands ... It's a very tough rule, this one: wash your hands before you start meal preparation or touching food or after handling raw meats before touching other foods. Or, for good measure, after sneezing into your hand.

Counter top thawing ... Is a no-no because meat thaws at a very slow pace from outside to inside, so while the inside is still merrily thawing, the outside is languishing in the (relative) heat, inviting bacteria to party – "Hey, come on over, have a seat, talk to me, just don't go downstairs – too cold." Instead, thaw it in your fridge, because, compared to your freezer, your fridge is the Bahamas, except without the harmful bacterial growing climate your room-temperature counter has. Or, use your microwave. The only thing about the microwave is that if you mistime your thawing on the plus side, you're cooking as well – something that can totally screw up the meal you're trying to make.

Leftover law ... It's easy to forget to put leftovers from dinner during parties or the playoffs into the fridge immediately, because there's so much going on. The fact is you should refrigerate hot foods as soon as possible – within two hours after cooking. If it's been standing out for more than two hours, pitch it. Don't bother trying to taste-test it, either. Even a small amount of contaminated food can cause illness. Date leftovers so they can be used within a safe time. Generally, they remain safe when refrigerated for three to five days. "If in doubt, throw it out." Reheat leftovers to at least 165º Fahrenheit. <u>Very important</u>. Bacteria can be eliminated by proper cooking and reheating – an easy way to stay out of the bathroom.

Unclean cutting board ... Cutting boards are one of those things that demand faith: you have to have faith the raw chicken you cut yesterday has entirely disappeared from its surface, that no salmonella potentialella (a new word, do you like it?) is lying in wait. It's kind of like jumping out of a plane with a parachute that *looks* like it's been properly packed. To the untrained eye, (the eye that may be looking into the toilet later on), the cutting board looks clean because it was rinsed of visual evidence of poultry presence, but is it? Negatory. What's the best way to clean it? Anti-bacterial agent, then rinsed. Or the dishwasher. Or, the 30-second hot water and soap program, as long as the water is hotter than hell.

Marinating at room temperature ... Most people know you can leave meat and fish out of the fridge for between 30–45 minutes while preparing to cook it. Some people, however, pull the meat out of the fridge, prepare it, put their meat/chicken/whatever into a marinade – and then leave it on the counter to marinate for hours. A BIG NG there, good buddy. Prepare your meat/chicken/ whatever, place it into the marinade, and then put it back in the fridge to marinate until you're ready to cook it (if you ever get confused about which is the verb and which is the noun, think of lemon*ade,* which, to my understanding, is also a noun).

Contaminated marinade ... Some people do everything right: they've stored their meat at the right temperature, they've properly refrigerated their meat in the marinade, and then, while they're barbequing, they gleefully brush on the marinade that's had the raw meat in it for the past 4 hours. Another NG. Make a little extra marinade and use it to baste instead.

Too long in the huddle between fridges ... You've got to be sensitive to how much time your groceries spend between refrigerators. If you have multiple stops to make, buy your perishables at your last stop. If you're doing your grocery shopping by public transit, ask for an insulated bag and freezer pak for your birthday, so your expensive meats and dairy products won't go to waste because the GD bus was late.

Raw & cooked meats on the same platter ... This is another one of those what-the-hell-was-I-thinking things. This is a very common occurrence every single barbequing season: someone buys great steaks, walks out to the BBQ, cooks them to perfection and places them back on the same plate they marched out on, which, unfortunately, contains the very bacteria cooking gets rid of. Kind of like a we're-back-to-square-one kind of thing.

Same spoon to stir and taste ... This has two unsavory ramifications:

1. The person doing the stirring/tasting is sharing whatever ailments they may have with whoever they're feeding, and

2. Whatever they're tasting may not be properly cooked or warmed up yet, exposing them to the bacteria cooking or reheating would kill.

Shared knife for raw meat and vegetables ... Can you say "cross-contamination"? Of course you can, and that's what you're doing. You're sharing whatever bacteria the meat has with whatever bacteria the vegetables have, and vice versa. And just who's the beneficiary of this cross-athon? Your gastrointestinal tract.

Reheating food ... Some people (take my 15-year-old son, for example), are so hungry and impatient, they reheat their food to the point where it no longer is cold. I'm finally getting it through to him that bacteria = bathroom, so Make it Bubble or Steam. It's supposed to be heated to 165 degrees Fahrenheit, but let's not be entirely anal about it. Just make sure it's steaming or bubbling like a madman. Need the heat to kill bacteria.

Can-fridged canned food ... If you don't finish what's in the can when you first open it, either transfer it to a fridge-worthy container, or drop back and punt. If you leave an opened tin of food in the fridge, oxidization occurs, a chemical reaction between the air and the metal – with your food an unwitting voyeur and you as the unwilling participant.

What else did Mom know that you should know?

Hamburger help ... E. coli has such an ugly ring to it, and an even uglier reality. Think of ground beef as E. coli's primary means of transportation, and the only way to make sure the bus doesn't stop at your home is to ensure your burgers are properly cooked. Regardless of how you like your burgers done, the safest way to cook them is until they are no longer red in the center and the juices run clear. Better yet, use a meat thermometer and cook to 160º F or 71º C. And don't even think of giving a child or senior a rare burger. Undercooked hamburgers cause more children to be ill every summer than swimming in Lake Erie. If you do not have a meat thermometer, don't eat ground beef patties that are still pink in the middle. Make life easier for yourself by stabbing the sucker with a meat thermometer and make sure it gets up to 160.

Do the dishes! ... The best way to do the dishes, from a bacteria-prevention standpoint, is to either do them in a dishwasher, or, if you don't have one yet, put them into hot water, wash them immediately (after immersion), rinse, and let them air dry. If you put dishes in the sink, let them soak for a couple of hours and then do them, you've unwittingly created dish soup, where the food has contributed to the main ingredient: bacteria. Also, the problem with hand towels is that bacteria get spread around, joyously.

Raw poultry, fish or meat handling ... Let's say you're making dinner; you take the chicken breasts out of the package, and put them in the dish for marinating. Then what? Wash your hands immediately with soap and warm water for 20 seconds. If you have a cut, best to wear rubber gloves.

Poultry, fish or meat defrosting ... It's good to know that smaller items will defrost more evenly than larger ones. Keep that in mind when packaging chicken breasts and hamburger. You should cook these thawed meats immediately after thawing. Incidentally, don't thaw poultry, meat and fish on the counter; bacteria get very amorous at room temperature and multiply too quickly.

Fruits and vegetables ... Don't eat potatoes with "eyes"– as they are roots that contain a natural chemical that helps the suckers grow but can actually make you (or your kids) sick.

Don't eat tomatoes that "leak" under any circum-stances. The leakage says there's bacteria present that can cause stomach upset and worse (read: bathroom trip).

Do wash every single vegetable as though a passing representative from the livestock committee urinated on it.

Bread   ... Although this is not really a food safety issue, it really is handy: keep your bread in the freezer if you find your bread keeps getting moldy. Frozen bread is fine for toast and is great for kids' lunches because it thaws so quickly.

Kitchen Safety

One of the first things Mom taught you as a kid when you were standing around in the kitchen was Kitchen Safety. Her chief reason or incentive for the lessons was that she didn't have the time to deal with the mess your blood would make, and linoleum was quite new back then, so they weren't sure of its stain-resistance properties.

Let's go through the very basics, which I know will make some people roll their eyeballs at how obvious they are, but hey, toast is a novel concept to a beginner:

Stove	Don't use the stove as another shelf in the kitchen and store/leave things on the elements so that they become such a fixture you forget to remove them when you turn on the oven.
	One of the elements, usually the back right element, is fed from the oven, meaning, if the oven is on, this element will feel like it's on: good for keeping something kind of warm after it's cooked, also good for burning things by accident (see above).
	Don't leave food cooking. If you have to dash out for a moment, turn it off. It's better to spoil food than spoil your entire home and that of your neighbors. Most kitchen fires occur because someone started heating fat or oil and forgot about it. Oil has a smoking point, and don't forget, where's there's smoke, there's ...
Handles	Assume the handle's hot – use an oven mitt, not a dishtowel. Why? Because the dishtowel gives you less protection when holding something hot and the protection stops very suddenly, so you'll be halfway to the table carrying your first tuna casserole, using a dishtowel, and suddenly you realize it's really HOT and you have an Indiana Jones moment: do you turn back or do you press on? But you look back to the

stove and forth to the table and you're exactly halfway, and either direction is getting farther and farther away, so your only recourse is ... to drop the GD casserole, distributing hot peas all over your feet. Bad scene. Get a proper oven mitt and assume whatever you're going to carry is going to be hot. Note: not SPRINT hot, just hot, as in, don't try to sprint across the dilapidated bridge to get there before it collapses.

Everyone knows the don't-leave-handles-sticking-out-where-young-children-and-clothing-may-yank-on-it rule of pot management, but don't go so crazy you spin the handle above another element you're using or close to that oven vent we discussed.

Fire

Water does not extinguish a grease fire; consider using baking soda, a lid, or, for the complete hell of it, have an ABC fire extinguisher handy (just don't store it above the stove!).

Resist the temptation to carry a burning pot to the sink – you might trip over a beer bottle and spread the fire.

Steam

For some reason, people tend to view steam as a benign entity, perhaps because they associate it with Thomas the Steam Engine, but beware when you're using your microwave oven or steaming your vegetables: steam can cause extreme burns. Open lids away from your face or any part of you that's exposed (I don't want to know).

Cans

Theoretically, you should cut the entire lid off, let it fall into the food you'd like to eat, dig it out and then off you go. Because I don't like having to root through my virginal food to retrieve the lid of a can that's been sitting around a grocery store, I tend to can-open all the way around until just before I've severed the lid, prop it open, empty the can, then fold the lid back down. This method, however, could be considered dangerous if you forget to fold the lid down. On the one hand, I'm happy that I don't have grocery store grossness in my food, but on the other hand I wouldn't want to be responsible for someone who forgot to push the lid back down and a few minutes later reached to get something and caused grave injury.

Utensils | The second biggest trouble a beginner can get into (after slicing open their forearm on the above-mentioned counter-mounted guillotine) is trying to reenact _MacGyver_. If you're not familiar with the old ABC program, it featured a guy who was a master at improvising; he could make a rocket out of a toilet paper roll and fill it with aerosol and fly to Cuba with it. As enticing as it sounds, we often try to do something with something that was intended for something else. Example? Opening a can with a fork. Using things for which they weren't intended takes too long, does a crappy job and can hurt you, so ask for whatever you need as a gift.

Knives | You can walk into most people's kitchen and instantly recognize they've got the two big cooking components: a fridge and a stove. What's the other component that's as important? A good knife. Can't do a damn thing without a knife, unless you're into some sort of Medieval culinary thing. But what sort of knife? For someone who's learning to become a finely tuned Domestic Engineer, the following knives are appropriate:

12" chef's knife ... (or if you have small hands, an 8" or 10") The key thing is that it must feel comfortable in your hand.

7" paring knife ... this is the knife you'd use for peeling an orange, etc.

12" serrated knife ... for bread

It's important to make sure your knives are sharp, so make sure you learn to keep them sharp (don't try to sharpen your serrated knife – won't work). It's also important to mention that a sharpening steel (it looks like a rat-tail file) cannot sharpen a dull knife. They're only intended to straighten the edge of an already sharp knife, but they can't sharpen a dull knife – something you see people trying to do quite frequently. Some knife facts:

- If your knife comes in a block, put the blade sharp side up, otherwise it will dull quicker.

- Sharp knives are safer knives – they require less pressure to cut through food.

- Don't leave knives in a drawer – they dull quickly and there's a danger of someone cutting themselves. If you don't have a wooden block, look for one of those magnet things you can put on the wall.

- Don't put a knife into a soapy sink and then walk away. Your roommate or child will get a very unpleasant surprise if they decide to give you a hand and finish washing the dishes.

- The point of the knife should remain on the cutting board throughout the chopping, so it forms a pivot point. You're far less likely to pivot onto your finger than if you were madly chopping away.

Keep the following in mind when choosing a knife:

Knife Basics ... It is best to buy a knife with a blade that was cut from a single piece of metal, with no beveling; one that you can see runs the entire length of the knife's handle. Don't buy knives with hollow-ground blades made by joining two sheets of metal; they may break easily.

MATERIAL	PROS/CONS
Carbon Steel:	PROS: Easier to sharpen or "take an edge."
	CONS: Loses sharpness quickly and can discolor from contact with acidic food (tomatoes)
Stainless Steel:	PROS: Stronger than carbon and does not discolor. Stays sharp.
	CONS: Difficult to sharpen
High Carbon SS:	PROS: Carbon allows the blade to get and keep a sharp edge; SS prevents discoloration.
High Carbon SS:	CONS: None.
Titanium:	PROS: Lighter and more durable than steel; holds an edge after extended use.
	CONS: None, except they can be expensive.
Ceramic:	PROS: Can hold an edge for years with little maintenance.
	CONS: Brittle and require diamond sharpening tools and can only be used on cutting boards as they'll cut right through dinnerware glaze – something the girlfriend's parents take a dim view of. And, they're expensive as hell.

Fridge Management

This is the sort of arcane knowledge that we wish we had as we're about to feed someone we care about, whose opinion is important, say, a date or parent, and we wonder if we can do what we're about to do, and we certainly can't ASK anybody. It's also the sort of thing that can have a huge bearing on how much time we spend in the bathroom reliving the 3-week-old Chinese take-out food we just ate. The number one thing established Home Engineers recommend? Label things that go into the fridge so you know if they're safe to eat. Unfortunately, I think that's a bit weenie-ish. I can't imagine having masking tape and a marker handy so I can jot down "TUESDAY APRIL 17" on an old margarine container. Why? Because it really isn't my personality. On the other hand, I recommend knowing when something is well past the safe punting distance, so

MY recommendation on this is to have a complete color-coded system with a legend you can put on the fridge. At least this shows you have a sense of humor to go along with your attention to detail. So, this is how it would look:

Blue:	Monday
Green:	Tuesday
White:	Wednesday
Purple:	Thursday
Yellow:	Friday

And so on. The trick, of course, could be to scratch Roman Numerals onto the top and then cross out after 5 days, the way you would if you were stranded on a desert island, just in case you had something that could go in the fridge longer than a week, something the above system doesn't really take into account, since most things have to be eaten within a week anyway. The point is to find a balance between necessity and enjoyment.

Proper fridge temperature ... A recent survey found that over 50% of Americans had fridge temperatures of 50 degrees Fahrenheit! So, stop wondering why everything tastes funny and turn your fridge down to 41º F (5º C).

How long things keep ... **Do** get foods into the fridge as soon as possible after cooking – even if they're still warm (just leave the container's lid unsealed until the food has chilled). Use a shallow container, as it will speed the cooling.

Don't refrigerate tomatoes, bananas, potatoes, onions.

Do refrigerate plums, peaches, only after they've ripened and sweetened on your counter.

Do refrigerate cantaloupes, honeydew and other melons, unless you plan to eat them within a few days.

- Don't store milk or eggs on the door.
- Discard deli meats after 5 days.
- Discard cooked pasta and pizza after 3–5 days.
- Cooked rice should be punted after 5 days.

What else?

PRODUCT	REFRIGERATOR 41 °F	FREEZER 0 °F
Fresh beef roast, steaks, chops, or ribs	3 to 5 days	6 to 12 months
Other meats (pork, chicken)	1 or 2 days	3 to 4 months
Cooked beef, soups, stews or casseroles	3 to 4 days	2 to 3 months
Store-cooked convenience meals	1 to 2 days	2 to 3 months
Broth (Campbell's)	10 days	2 to 3 months
Beef hot dogs or lunch meats, unopened	2 weeks	1 to 2 months
Hot dogs, opened package	7 days	1 to 2 months
Lunchmeats, opened package	3 days	1 to 2 months
Condiments (opened)		
Mayonnaise	3 months	
Mustard	7 months	
Ketchup	5 months	
Cream cheese	2 weeks	
Ranch dressing	2 months	
Peanut butter	4 months	
Pickles	6 months	
Sour cream	3 weeks	
Blue cheese dressing	2 months	
Relish	6 months	
Gravy	3 days	
Soya sauce	1 year	
Margarine	4-5 months	

Know How to Plan Like a Mother

There are two key elements to learning to plan like a mother.

1. Budgets are kept within. Period.
2. Food is purchased based on what's nutritionally required by the family, not by what the kids demand (or what you demand if you shop hungry and plan-less!)

Creating a budget is not an easy task; there's no hard and fast rule that you have to spend X percentage of income on food, but only you can decide how much you're going to spend. Once you have a budget, you can plan. It's really easy to argue that a lack of planning leaves one vulnerable to the "what shall I make for dinner tonight, oh, here are some chips, I'll have a couple while I look in the cupboard, but damn, I'm hungry and eff it, I don't know what to make so I'll finish the chips." If this happens once in a while, it's kind of ok, but if you want a blueprint for how to gain weight and lose healthiness, that's it.

So, if we can somehow learn to be meal planners, we'll save money and eat better – two fairly strong incentives.

How do we plan? I'm not going to go into any great dissertation on nutrition, so let's just go with what our mothers knew: we have to eat a balanced diet. Which means, in almost every single dinner we're going to have representatives from the protein, carb and vegetable families:

Available proteins		Available carbs	Available vegetables
chicken	Whole roast Legs/thigh/breast	bread	broccoli
turkey	*	rice	cauliflower
pork	Chops, cutlets roasts	potatoes tortillas	carrots green beans
beef	Ground, veal, Steaks, roasts stewing		green peas onions squash
fish	tuna salmon haddock halibut		zucchini tomato corn lettuce peppers celery

* I have to mention something here. The Turkey Marketing people have been trying for ages to make people use turkey at times other than Thanksgiving or Christmas, but I'm not sure I buy it. I've tried buying turkey breasts and using them as chicken. I even tried buying ground turkey and including it in a recipe that called for it. I'm sorry to say, didn't work too well. May work for you, of course. They say it is a healthier version of chicken, but I couldn't manage it. So good luck. On the other hand, if it were so obviously more affordable, like almost half the price, you'd have to be an idiot to avoid it. Anyway, we're not talking about us yet; we're talking about Mom.

I know this is a really rudimentary list, it's kind of like teaching someone to drive: you have to know the rules before you can explain how to break them safely. I'm not going to list exotic or specialty foods, a) because I'm a basic kind of guy and don't really know them, and b) if you're sufficiently interested after you've become a competent domestic engineer, YOU can ask. The challenge is to start thinking along lines we may not be comfortable thinking in.

So, once we know the basic choices (the available protein/carbs /vegetables) and the basic premise (figure out basic meals for the week), you could have this meal plan:

Day	Protein	Carb	Vegetable
MONDAY	pork chops	Lipton SideKicks	broccoli
TUESDAY	salmon filet	white rice	carrots
WEDNESDAY	ground beef	pasta	peppers/celery /onion
THURSDAY	tuna	pasta	peas
FRIDAY	PIZZA!	PIZZA!	PIZZA!
SATURDAY	ground beef	pasta	onion/tomatoes
SUNDAY	Roast chicken	potatoes	green beans

In the chapter **Stuff to Make it With,** there is an outline of products that are considered staples. It's a good idea to go through that list and make your own list of what you have to have in your kitchen that will allow you to make the most amount of your favorite meals. So, each week when you're sitting down to do your list, make sure you take a look in your fridge, pantry and cupboards for staples – things you're going to buy regardless of whether they're on sale, but will buy more of if indeed they are on sale.

At this point, while you have an ideal (meaning, perfect for you) meal plan for the week, it doesn't yet reflect whether the store is having sales on things you're looking for. Now, before you start your shopping, prepare a shopping list broken down into four vertical columns (we're only talking about dinner here, I'm thinking you're all right with dessert decisions):

Staples	Protein	Carb	Veg
Frozen vegetables	Pork chops	Fast & Fancy Rice	broccoli*
Minute Rice	Fish (salmon)	small potatoes	green pepper
Flavored Rice	Ground beef	canned corn	celery
Pasta sauce	Canned tuna		green onions
Onions	Whole chicken		
Dry pasta			
Ground beef			
Cooking soups			
(Cream of broccoli)			
Potatoes			
Carrots			
Spices			

*   If you live in a climate that requires a bank loan to buy fresh produce come wintertime, the frozen broccoli and garden vegetables are really good these days – they used to be obviously frozen and regardless of what you did, they ended up on your plate limp and tasteless. Now, however, frozen vegetables are great and can be steamed very successfully. For a taste treat, if you have an indoor grill or a BBQ, you can put them in aluminum foil (sprinkle some herbs and spices on them, like garlic salt and oregano, for example), wrap it up and chuck it on the grill. They'll steam in their own liquids. It's good. Use brand name frozen vegetables, like **Green Giant**, rather than the generic ones, mainly because Green Giant seems to have a better grasp on what part of the vegetable we really want to eat, rather than a frozen piece of something we have to believe was once associated with a recognized vegetable. The only thing I can't get a frozen vegetable to do is go for a wok – really doesn't work – you need fresh for a wok.

But the key is to give some thought to what you'd like to eat the following week – thought along the lines of what you can afford and what is healthy for you. This way, you're not tempted by what may have enormous appeal at the moment (a loaf of fresh bread) but won't help you, nutritionally.

How to Shop Like a Mother

First, I want you to be aware that research says even *with* a list, over 60% of what we purchase will be impulse items. That said, however, you don't have to rely on the "seefood" approach to shopping.

So, you've got your list of *categories* based on meal requirements. You know you need certain proteins, carbs and vegetables for the meals you'd like to have the coming week. To complete your transformation from domestically-averse to domestically advanced, you now have to match your requirements with what's on sale. It would be easy to argue it's better to wait to see the flyers before creating your list, something that would take less time. You could probably do it either way, with seeing the flyers being a little quicker. Frankly, I think it boils down to your budget: if your primary goal is to eat a certain way and you can afford to buy things regardless of whether they're on sale, do your list first. If, on the other hand, you're on a tight budget, you'd be better off waiting to see the flyers and then creating a list following the four categories.

The important thing to remember is we're trying to eat well and save a little money while we're at it. Becoming shopping weenies, the ones that have a master shopping list they've photocopied and taped to the inside of their cupboard door so they can keep track of things they need on an on-going basis (although, damn, I wish I was that organized), is not the goal, so there are certain things we can do that will be our version of weenieism.

I'd like to say we could organize our shopping list according to how grocery stores flow, but since most grocery stores have a different flow (although most of them will have produce first, then bakery, then meat, and so on), my logic will be fairly loose. I think it's better to have a calm sense of purpose when grocery shopping; no one likes a highly focused shopping weenie, although it's equally amusing to see someone standing in the middle of the bulk food section with a vacuous look as they try to remember what they came for.

But it is important to bear in mind that even for a college student with just one person to be concerned about, there are staples to keep stocked and shopping traps to avoid, such as forgetting to buy a staple at a grocery store and having to buy it at a convenience store for 145% of the price you could have paid. Do that once a week for the entire school year and you could have bought an extra case of beer or a dinner out per month.

Great. So now you've started thinking about what you should eat and planning your meals based on how much money you have and a nutritional guideline. Now what? Do you just march to your grocery store and gleefully pick up the first thing that fits the description on your list? Well, you could, but it wouldn't be very motherly. There are two key cost-saving things to consider:

1. Flyers
2. Unit price

Flyers

The next step of planning like a mother is taking a peek through your neighborhood grocery store's flyer – if you haven't already. On second thought, if you have to drive a little further to get to a superstore, and you can justify the added travel expense, there's no question you'll save money at a superstore. Think about it. Generally every single week a big store will offer a terrific saving on something within one of your columns. For example, last week I went shopping for a roast beef, which was going to cost me $18 for the number of people I had to feed. But, the store had a sale on a pork roast for $11. So, we had pork.

I know from experience how difficult it is to adjust to behavior that isn't innate: looking through flyers. But it's almost tragic to avoid the weekly savings these flyers will alert you to. Don't expect to see all the sales while at the store – unless you enjoy walking around like an idiot, tripping over all the other wankers who didn't take the time to look through the store flyer. That said, of course, keep your eye out for sales – within the four staples columns shown above, primarily, and secondarily for things you'll need. I know it sounds completely stupid: no one should need shopping help, but the fact is you can save a quarter of your food budget and eat better. You're probably thinking, "I look through flyers, I never see anything good!" And you're probably right, but it may be you're looking through them with the wrong criteria in mind or you have nothing in mind and you're just looking through them. I can say that because I used to look through grocery store flyers if I had nothing else to read and the sporting goods store flyer hadn't been delivered yet.

The trick to looking through these flyers is to see each product not just as a stand-alone product, but how it relates to the meals you like to eat. Looking crazily for pork but chicken's on sale? Cool, you're having chicken. Looking for frozen vegetables but canned vegetables are on sale? Cool, you're having canned vegetables. And bear in mind, you fresh vegetable snob, that you don't necessarily have to have these canned vegetables on the side of your plate looking very out-of-a-can, you can make a casserole or sauce with them.

Unit Price

There used to be a time when you had to carry a calculator around the grocery store to determine unit pricing – the best way of seeing if something is a smart buy, or not. Most grocery stores (I think it's the law now, whereas before it used to be sheer thoughtful consideration on their part) have a card that indicates unit price on the shelf in front of each product. You know, when you look at a product that costs $3.28 for 12 oz and the next one is $4.78 for 16 oz and you're trying to figure out what the better deal is. The first card might say

Product:	**Heinz Deep Browned Beans**
Price:	$3.28
Size:	12 oz
Unit Price:	$0.27/oz

Having the unit price card is a beautiful thing if you majored in English and there's a math-related reason for your choice of major, as these cards do the comparisons for you. You look at the store brand and you might see

Product:	**Store Brand Deep Browned Beans**
Price:	$4.78
Size:	16 oz
Unit Price:	$0.29/oz

This is great to know because you can buy the smaller one with confidence, knowing you didn't pay a huge premium for the smaller size. This way, also, you can waltz around the store, merrily looking for deals. It's probably the most useful when you're considering something that's normally way too expensive but is on sale and you're wondering just how much of a deal it is: compare the unit price with the brand you normally buy; you'll find in a lot of cases it's still way more expensive than your usual brand.

This is important when you want to compare national brands against store brands. The misconception is that the store brands will always be cheaper, but this is not always the case – sometimes it's nuts how much more the unit price is for a store brand.

Size Matters to everyone

This may seem like a small thing, but make sure you're comparing apples to apples in terms of size. Sometimes when we're in a hurry and we're looking for pasta sauce and the national brand is $2.50 for 16 oz and the store brand is only $2.25, we buy a couple, not noticing that the store brand size is actually 15 oz. Be sure to look. Speaking of looking, make sure you're comparing apples to apples regarding unit price, as in, make sure the unit of measurement is the same.

Label Reading

Sometimes having the right information at the right time makes all the difference. Food companies are now following their store compatriots by providing information that may influence our decision to purchase, information such as how many calories are derived from fat, what percentage of the recommended daily allowance of vitamins it contains, etc. However, the label can be a little daunting because there are so many things they're trying to accomplish with the food labels. Food labels have two sections. The top section contains product-specific information such as serving size, nutritional info and calories.

This is a sample label for Macaroni & Cheese:

Nutrition Facts
Serving Size 1 cup (228g)
Serving Per Container 2

Start here first –
will it feed the number
of people you have to
feed?

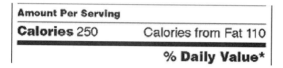

Amount Per Serving

Calories 250   Calories from Fat 110

% Daily Value*

Be very aware of foods
that derive a high
percentage of total
calories from Fat.

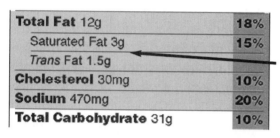

Total Fat 12g	18%
Saturated Fat 3g	15%
Trans Fat 1.5g	
Cholesterol 30mg	10%
Sodium 470mg	20%
Total Carbohydrate 31g	10%

For health,
limit these fats.

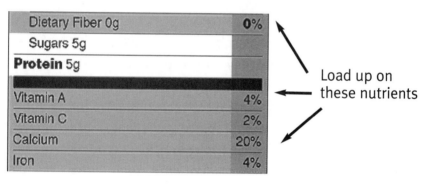

Dietary Fiber 0g	0%
Sugars 5g	
Protein 5g	
Vitamin A	4%
Vitamin C	2%
Calcium	20%
Iron	4%

Load up on
these nutrients

Bear in mind that the Percent Daily Values are based on a standard
2,000-calorie diet. Individual Daily Values may be lower or higher,
of course, depending on your goals. Regardless of goals, however,
for health purposes, follow these guidelines:

1. Pay attention to the serving size, eg., are you really
   only going to have one cup?
2. Pay equal attention to the Calories from Fat, meaning,
   if over 50% of the product's calories are from fat, that
   product will indeed contribute to your size. Health
   experts feel you should get less than 30% of your total
   daily calories from fat.

3. Pay even closer attention to the types of fat*.
4. Some people are concerned about salt intake, so they watch the Sodium level.
5. All things being equal, look for products that have a good Nutrient representation (Vitamin A, C, Calcium, etc.)

Lastly, regarding the % Daily Values, it's also appropriate to know what's considered high and low. We know by now we're seeking high (20% or more) values in nutrients – dietary fiber – but it's also important to know we're seeking low values of sugars, calories.

* Since we're on the topic of fats, let's lift the blubber and take a quick peek into what the researchers are saying now. This section has more meat to it because of contributions by my nephew, Michael Kennedy, Director of Operations for At Work Health Solutions. Since this is not a science or medicine book, I'm not going to go into the fairly involved explanation of cholesterol and lipoproteins, but I can tell you what the Harvard School of Public Health says about fats:

Saturated Fats are primarily animal fats. These are kind of good news/bad news fats, as they are known to raise both good cholesterol (HDL) and bad (LDL). In the past, it was recommended to limit these types of fats in your diet, something that is now in question because of the weight loss effectiveness of high protein diets. I personally think it's best to avoid these types of fats, but, hey, who the hell am I? Go for high protein/lower fat meats, if you're bent on the high protein, low carb diets.

Trans Fats. By now you probably know these are the fats that are banned in most intelligent countries, or at least limited. In North America, we're consuming 5 times the daily suggested allowance of unhealthy fats – with trans fats leading the charge. Trans fats occurs by hydrogenation, where unsaturated fat is processed to become more saturated, something that increases the shelf life of processed foods. Introducing hydrogen to liquid vegetable oil that is being heated, produces hydrogenated oils, or trans fats. You may have noticed that saturated fats, like butter or the fat from a roast, are solid at room temperature, while unsaturated fat, like olive oil, are liquid. By "saturating" or injecting an unsaturated fat with hydrogen, it will act like a saturated fat. These Trans Fats are the evil stepsisters because not only do they raise the crappy cholesterol (LDL), they take out the helpful cholesterol (HDL) in the process.

Unsaturated Fats – polyunsaturated and monounsaturated – are considered good fats because they can improve blood cholesterol levels. So, cooking oils that derive a high percentage of their fats from *mono- and polyunsaturated* fats are the healthiest choice. This is why most experts feel safflower, olive oil and canola oils are good choices for cooking, because they get the majority of their fat from monounsaturated fat and polyunsaturated fat.

The disheartening thing, for someone like me who's a collar-wearing cookie hound, is that it's almost impossible to escape the words "hydrogenated, partially hydrogenated oil or vegetable oil shortening" on the package of anything you like to eat. And it's not a matter of whether you choose Dare's Major Triple Maniac Chocolate cookies or the most benign of all biscuits, Arrowroots: they both have hydrogenated oils[†]. Period.

So, although it's very difficult to avoid, you still have to be aware of it: if you see the words "hydrogenated, partially hydrogenated, hydrogenated, or saturated fats" or some variation on that theme, on something you're considering eating, be aware you are consuming something remarkably harmful to your health. Why? Because according to The Harvard School of Public Health, there is a real, clear link between the types of fat you consume and heart disease – with trans fats – the ones in all your cookies, chips and crackers –being the worst, flabby hands down.

† Note: this may have changed since publication. Snack and cookie manufacturers are under intense pressure to eliminate these harmful fats, but some move faster than others.

How to Cook Like a Mother

OK, now we can plan, shop, save and know what we're buying. Now what? We'd better know the basic terms that will be referred to in recipes.

Basic Terms

Aging	applies to meat being refrigerated between 34–36 degrees Fahrenheit, to make meat more tender
Al dente	more chewy ("would you like your pasta al dente or well cooked?")
Baste	to pour drippings, fat or stock over food while cooking
Batter	a thin flour mixture that can be poured or dropped
Blanched	to scald briefly (cleans and livens up taste)
Boil	bring a liquid or mixture to a full bubbling motion
Braising	a cooking method where food is first browned in oil, then cooked slowly in liquid – wine, stock or water
Browning	refers to the point where the meat is no longer pink inside
Broil	cook under direct heat
C	cup
Chop	cut into small uneven pieces
Dice	cut into small even cubes
Divided	if a recipe asks for, say, 5 teaspoons of a seasoning, divided, it means do them one measurement at a time, not all whacked together
Garnish	decorate
Fry	cooking method using little or no fat in a fry pan or skillet
Grate	shred
Grill	cooking method where a grill suspends meat over heat
Heat	high, medium or low
Julienne	cut into long, thin strips
Kosher	meat that is butchered and processed according to Hebrew religious laws

Oz	ounce
Pan-broiling	to cook in an uncovered fry pan so the fat can be poured off while cooking.
Panfry	same as stir-fry, but in a pan rather than a wok
Parboiling	cook partially by boiling for a short period of time
Peel	remove outer skin
Poach	method of cooking primarily fish where the food is cooked in liquid
Pot roast	cooking method involving less expensive cuts of meat, cooked with ample liquid
Reduce	to concentrate a liquid by extensive simmering
Sauté	cook in a small amount of oil or fat with constant stirring
Sear	scorch or brown the surface of meat to seal in juices
Simmer	cook liquid below the boiling point
Slice	cut crosswise
Stir-fry	cooking method, usually in a wok, that involves constant movement of food to maximize exposure to heat, resulting in quick cooking and flavor retention
Stock	the broth in which meat, fish, bones, or vegetables are simmered for a relatively long period, used as a base in preparing soup, gravy, or sauces.
Tender	a fork will enter with little resistance
Tbsp or T	tablespoon
Tsp or t	teaspoon
Tenderloin	a piece of very tender meat, refers to beef, pork, lamb and veal
Toss	a method of mixing that is done with two spoons or forks using a lifting motion and is meant to avoid causing the physical damage to delicate food that stirring would cause
Translucent	clear

You'll want to remember those terms for the recipe reading section later on. I found it was difficult to read recipes not knowing what the hell they were talking about.

Timing and temperatures

A frequent gripe by students in my Cooking for the Domestically Challenged cooking class is "I can never get everything to be ready at the same time – I'm always having to wait for something and everything else gets cold!" This, to my way of thinking, is a combination of not knowing how long things take to cook and not taking the time to properly consider when you want them to be cooked. The first time you cook for a group of people is probably the first time you'll give consideration to cooking times. And, the first time you eat an hour and a half late because you effed up the timing and everyone's hammered and throwing things and tripping over the dog, is the last time you will take a casual approach to mealtime planning, I can assure you.

So, what follows is the cooking time for various proteins and vegetables, but right off the bat you have to be thinking about what time you really want to eat. Think in terms of this grid, assuming you want to eat at 6:00 pm:

	Meat	Vegetables	Carbs	Bread (heated)
Cooking Time	3.5 hours	20 mins	45 mins	5 minutes
Start Time**	2:15pm*	5:40pm	5:15pm	5:55pm

** Allowing a roast to sit for 10 or so minutes before carving is recommended.
* People get screwed up because they don't account for the prep time; all they're thinking about is the cooking time. So, if something's going to take 15 minutes to cook, but it takes 10 minutes to prepare, you're going to eat 10 minutes late, unless you factor that in. Same thing for the roast: if you want to eat at 6 and you know it's going to take 3.5 hours and you start *preparing* the roast at 2:15, again, you're going to eat late because you didn't account for the prep time.

There's no question that the first few times you do a larger than average-scale dinner, you're going to have to write down a timing grid – unless you've very smart. Moms can do it the same way my Dad could look at a screw and tell me its thread count and size. So, the two keys:

1. have a timing plan or grid
2. factor in the prep time so you don't get frustrated, annoyed or hammered – or all three.

These are guidelines, because the best thing you can do for yourself or anyone you're cooking for is to get a meat thermometer, which eliminates the old "gee, it looked cooked and it should have been cooked," which you're plaintively muttering through the bathroom door. If you're someone with a healthy level of skeptical curiosity, you can "calibrate" your meat thermometer by inserting it into boiling water. If it reads 212° F, you're in business.

Let's start with fish. Cookbooks refer to a fish-cooking "10-minute rule," a rule that means you cook for 10 minutes per inch of fish.

Baking   You can bake whole fish, fillets, steaks and hunks of fish. Use pieces of similar size for even cooking. Use a preheated, 450° F oven, with the 10-minute rule, bake uncovered, baste (optional).

Broiling   You can bake whole fish, fillets, steaks and hunks of fish. Use pieces of similar size for even cooking. Use a preheated, 450° F oven, with the 10-minute rule, bake uncovered, baste (optional).

Grilling   This technique is popular for fish such as salmon, halibut, swordfish, and tuna. Preheating your grill is important. Bear in mind skin is reluctant to stick to a clean and oiled grill.

                To avoid your steaks and fillets drying out during grilling, baste steaks and fillets while grilling. Try marinating fish about an hour before grilling to keep it moist. Don't forget the 10-minute rule for doneness.

Recommended Cooking Temperatures, Internal Temperatures and Cooking Times for various meats

Food	°F	°C
Ground Meat & Meat Mixtures		
Beef, Pork, Veal, Lamb	160	71
Turkey, Chicken	170	77
Fresh Beef, Veal, Lamb		
Medium Rare	145	63
Medium	160	71
Well Done	170	77
Poultry		
Chicken & Turkey, whole	180	82
Poultry breasts, roast	180	82
Poultry thighs, wings	180	82
Stuffing (cooked alone or in bird)	165	74
Fresh Pork		
Medium	160	71
Well Done	170	77
Ham		
Fresh (raw)	160	71
Pre-cooked (to reheat)	140	60
Seafood	145	63
Eggs & Egg Dishes		
Eggs	Cook until yolk & white are firm	
Egg dishes	160	71
Leftovers & Casseroles	165	74

Cooking Times for Vegetables

These cooking times reflect if you boil them. You can use the same times if you steam them, or roughly half of these times if you cook them in the microwave. My concern about using the microwave is a recent story by Dutch researchers that said they found heavy nutrient and vitamin drop-off in microwaved broccoli versus steaming, so if I wasn't a fan of steamed vegetables before, I am now. The following table is only a guideline – you have to bear in mind there are really no hard and fast times – because of the variance in heat, pot thickness, integrity of cover, etc. I think the best way is to use the following guide, but keep testing the vegetables until they have the texture you like – then at least you'll know the next time.

Steamer: Make sure the water is equal to the bottom of the actual steamer (if it has legs). Also, make sure you have a decently fitting lid.

Microwave: Only use a splash of water (supposed to be 3 tablespoons, but, come on, who cares, put in a small splash).

And, most important, bear in mind you can always cook vegetables a little longer; you can't un-cook an overdone vegetable.

Fresh Vegetables (Minimum amounts)	Cooking Time	Water
Asparagus, thick whole	5 minutes	½ cup
Beans, green or wax	5 minutes	½ cup
Broccoli, flowers	4-5 minutes	½ cup
Broccoli, spears	7-8 minutes	½ cup
Brussels sprouts, large (fresh)	10-12 minutes	¾ cup
Brussels sprouts, small	4-5 minutes	¾ cup
Carrots, 1-inch chunks	10-12 minutes	¾ cup
Cauliflower, florets	6-8 minutes	½ cup
Corn on the cob	6-8 minutes (until you can smell it!)	

Fresh Vegetables (Minimum amounts)	Cooking Time	Water
Mixed Vegetables, Frozen	6 minutes	½ cup
Potatoes, new, or small (2 oz), whole	15-18 minutes	1 cup
Potatoes, whole	40-45 minutes	1 cup
Spinach, coarsely chopped	3 minutes	½ cup
Squash, acorn, halved	25 minutes	1 cup
Squash, butternut, 1-inch pieces	10 minutes	¾ cup
Squash, spaghetti, approx. 2 pounds, whole	10 minutes	1 ½ cups
Sweet potato, 1 ½" pieces	12 minutes	1 cup
Turnips, 1 ½" pieces	12 minutes	½ cup

Recipe Reading

If we consider cooking as a science, a science that expects certain reactions, relative to when and for how long things take to occur, we can begin to understand why recipes seem confusing. ("Why should I do this now? Is the order of this recipe necessary or arbitrary?") With the terms mentioned above, it should be a breeze.

Your Basic Run of the Mill Standard Issue Spaghetti

What you'll Need

1 tablespoon. olive oil
1 cup chopped onion
2 cloves garlic, minced
½ lb ground beef
1 16 oz. can tomato sauce
1 green pepper, cut into strips
1-½ cups water
1 teaspoon. salt
1 teaspoon. dried basil
¼ teaspoon. pepper
4 oz. uncooked spaghetti pasta, broken in half

The ingredients and actions are listed in the order they are used. In this case, the olive oil goes in the pan first, the pan is brought up to heat, followed by adding the onions and the garlic.

What You'll Do

1. Wash your hands.
2. Over medium heat, heat olive oil in fry pan then add onion and garlic.
3. Sauté until translucent.
4. Add ground beef and cook and stir until beef is browned and vegetables are tender.
5. Stir in remaining ingredients except for uncooked spaghetti.
6. Bring to a boil, reduce heat, and put timer on to simmer for 25 minutes.
7. Add uncooked spaghetti to the simmering sauce a little at a time, stirring to keep it separated. Cover tightly and let simmer over low heat or until pasta is tender, stirring frequently, probably about 10 minutes.

It's important to do as you would for Ikea instructions or assembling a barbeque: read the instructions all the way through from beginning to end. This way you will know that you have all the ingredients and tools on hand. You will also be able to look up recipe terms you don't understand so cooking proceeds smoothly.

Sometimes the preciseness of recipes turns people off, so while measurements in recipes can be critical, let's assume a more reasonable stance on this: if you know what the stated quantity is supposed to be, let your personality dictate exactly how much goes in. It's your decision.

An important thing to realize is a recipe writer is trying to be very precise with language because quantities (the above notwithstanding, of course) dictate the outcome. For example, if the recipe says

1 cup cranberries, chopped

it means measure one cup of cranberries, then chop the mothers. If it says

1 cup chopped cranberries

it means you should end up with a cup of chopped cranberries, which will take more than a cup of unchopped berries.

Same thing for onions. The recipe may call for 1 onion, chopped. Big difference if it calls for 1 cup of chopped onion. Even the order of words in a recipe ingredient list changes the preparation of the foods.

When it's time to cook the pasta, bear in mind most pasta will not take longer than 20 minutes, and to test it, remove one piece and, once cooled, test it. Don't try the throw the pasta against the wall thing unless you are very fond of eating dust.

It's also important to keep in mind that frequent stirring is more often the norm, so don't stray too far from the kitchen. Lastly, cooking times mentioned in recipes, unless given to you by friends and families from their family favorites, were established for the most part in test kitchens, probably under the best conditions you could find. So, build some tolerance into the recipe. A common reaction to a burnt or undercooked meal is "Well, I followed EXACTLY what the recipe said!" That's no consolation to those eating, so be prepared for your stove to have different cooking times than the one whoever wrote the recipe used.

Good Things to Know

Good cooks are efficient. They can make decisions based on what they want to do or achieve, using whatever tools, utensils, ingredients or cookware they feel will get the job done. Good cooking is all about efficiency; it's challenging enough to make good (healthy) cooking choices, it's almost an insurmountable challenge if everything you'd like to do requires enormous effort because you can't find what you're looking for – or it's dirty. You know, when you're doing an infrequent job or task and half the time is spent getting things organized or getting enough things out of the way to get at the actual task? Or when you require a tool that's at the back of your garage, but your cousin Vinny's storing his stuff there – "for just a few months," and now the task of actually getting to the tool you need has become an Olympic Search and Rescue Op? One that requires the balance of a 78-lb, 12-year-old gymnast to get to where you think the tool should be and then requires the strength of a Pro Bowl offensive lineman to clear the spot? That's what I mean.

We're trying to avoid those times in your kitchen when you have to go so far out of your way just to do something right, that you'll either forget what you were doing or you'll say a resounding "eff it." The following is a list of things that will allow you to make the decisions you want, not the decisions you have to make because things are just too onerous to do:

Have a container ... for fat, one with a lid, which you can keep under the sink. Otherwise, when you make bacon or a meal with ground beef – and you want to drain the fat but you can't find a container and everyone's yelling at you that they're late – chances are you'll consume the extra fat. (And you know you shouldn't just pour it down the drain because it will congeal and clog the drain. Having a clogged drain – either in your sink or your body – doesn't sound like much fun and is a pain to have repaired.)

Clean as you go ... Meaning, don't leave a kitchen festooned with dirty knives and plates, so you can't put anything on the counter because there's just too much crap. Good cooks prepare, put away, prepare, put away. Again, it's like tools: get into the habit of putting your tools and all the stuff you're using back where it belongs.

Ever walk ... into your grandmother's house and use the peeler but not return it to the exact spot you got it from? Are your ears still ringing? The apparently over-the-top reaction you got was not necessarily a hallmark of a senior, it was also the hallmark of a good cook: they know where everything is. Why is this important?

If you're a sailor, you know the answer: when you need something, you need it NOW. Of course, if you can't find the garlic press it doesn't mean you're going to end up on a reef, but it does mean you have to slow down and consider the options – all of which takes extra time or takes away the taste you're trying to add since you'll probably just blow off the extra time and chuck the garlic. So, make your life easier: organize your kitchen. Know where things go and be consistent about where you put things.

Spices: The When and Why

Spices are a funny thing and can be a mystery to domestic newcomers. It's easy to have a profound respect for them, as, don't forget, they were a primary incentive 400 years ago for people to risk their lives traveling to places a) they hoped exist, and b) they hoped had these exotic spices, and c) they could get back from. Imagine if the space program was created because Mars was believed to have some really whacked-out spices? Getting them is one thing; knowing how to use them is indeed another thing altogether. Furthermore, because spices and herbs – their makeup and amounts – are so complex, they can be someone's life's work. Great chefs are created or deleted because of what they do with herbs and spices. (For a complete list of recommended herbs and spices, see **Stuff to Make it With**.)

That said, how can we become wise beyond our capabilities when it comes to herbs/spices?

First, some rules:

☞ Crush leaf herbs in your hands to activate and release the flavors.

☞ Don't hold a lid in one hand and shake your seasoning with the other hand into the pot. Why? What happens if the GD little dispenser thing falls off and you now have a mountain of special herbs and spices sitting on top of your stew, all set to pull an Atlantis? Save the mythology – and the stew: sprinkle your seasonings into your hand and distribute from there.

Here's a rundown of the when's – when you should add your carefully chosen herbs and spices – and the why's.

☞ If you want to enhance or maximize the herb/spice flavor, add them near the end of cooking.

☞ If you want your house to smell homey, add them right off the bat, especially while you're sautéing something.

☞ If you want the herbs and spices to have a gentler flavor, add them near the beginning.

☛ There's no set standard for how spices and herbs perform, so start with a small amount first and keep adding. It's kind of like someone who reaches for the saltshaker before they've tasted their food – make sure it needs it!

Gems

Once you've made a few meals and you've gotten good at them, you're ready to do what Moms do: add one step that makes the difference. It's generally the step that elevates the meal from "this is good, honey," to "ooooh, honey, come over here!"

All I can really do is list a number of Gems that I use and their respective uses. They're really very simple, but they make a difference.

Stock — A tin of powdered stock, whether it's chicken, vegetable or beef makes an unbelievable difference. Say you're steaming vegetables; add a snort of vegetable or chicken stock to the water. Making beef stew but are a little low on the meat budget? Add some beef stock to your stew. Same thing for pasta sauce. Using stock as a complement to meals when you can only afford a little of primary meat, makes up the difference in taste.

Red wine — Since we're on the topic of beef stew, or pot roast or pasta sauce, add a little (note, I said little) red wine. White wine can be added to meals involving chicken or fish, but doesn't seem to have the dramatic effect on taste adding red wine does.

Browning to the burnt point ... The whole concept of browning can be a little misleading. If the recipe says brown something, you could stop at that exact moment, but I've found if you bring it to the point where you see some of the meat is very cooked, the overall taste is more intense. You'll have to experiment, though.

Al dente vegetables ... The reverse applies for vegetables, at least in my household. Vegetables that are mushy and overcooked are vegetables that aren't very popular, so try your best to undercook vegetables in the beginning – you can always cook them longer if you keep losing a filling. You shouldn't be distracted by how crunchy the vegetables are; I'm just trying to warn against cases of wimpy and mushy vegetables. I'm referring, by the way, primarily to those inside sauces.

Oil and spice roasts ... When I first started making roasts, I was happy if they came out of the oven cooked and looking decent – brown and all that. I then discovered that if you do as they suggest, lightly coat a whole chicken with olive oil and add spices like a fiend, the result is much better. Doing so, of course, calls for a basting brush, something that borders on the weenie, but having one is worth it, I can now attest.

Tasty toast Sometimes it's knowing what to do with things we have everyday that makes it Mom-Like. Try this with toast (if you have a toaster oven):

1. Spread margarine (non-hydrogenated!) or butter on bread.
2. Sprinkle on some parmesan cheese – enough to cover the bread lightly.
3. Sprinkle on some oregano, then some garlic salt.
4. Toast – in a toaster oven!

Gems are what will make your meals transcend from the day-to-day stuff to what even you look forward to making and eating. So, keep your eye open when you're home for the holidays or near an accomplished cook – they may give away a secret without meaning to!

What's For Dinner: Recipes

One Pot Wonders
Great taste at great haste

Weekday Whackers
Whack it together in a hurry

Famous Forkers
Recognizable Repasts

Sides and Sauces
Mom Did 'em Now You Can Do 'em!

One Pot Wonders:
Great Taste at Great Haste

Or is it, Great Haste with Great Taste? Or, Great Taste IN Great Haste? Or … who cares. Either way, here's a list of meals that will satisfy your tummy and respect your timing. All measurements are intended for a group of 3–4 people, unless stated otherwise. The main criteria for these meals is that they end up being meals our Moms *could* have made: they're comforting, tasty and nutritious – and we're not compromising taste just because we have to make them in great haste. To keep the meat fatigue to a minimum, these recipes represent the best in a field of many. And don't forget, while casseroles wouldn't normally be considered pots, if it's quick and doesn't require too much screwing around and it starts and ends in the casserole dish, it's here.

Beef	Hamburger Heaven
	Pre-PC Corn
	Burger Stroganoff
	Hangover Corned Beef Hash
	Cindy's Shipwreck Beef Casserole
	Baked Putanesca Heaven
Chicken	Murphy's Serendipitous Chicken
	Chicken Strips and Vegetable Stir Fry
	Cheesy Chicken
	Pie-free Chicken Pot Pie
Pork	Baggie's Pork Stew
	Pork Chop Stew
Fish	Tuna Casserole

This is a big hit because it tastes great and is very comforting; the fact it's healthy provides an added bonus.

What you'll need:
small splash olive oil (2 tablespoons if you're the precise type)
1 chopped clove of garlic, if you're ambitious and have the time
1 medium onion
½ lb lean ground beef
½ each, one green and one red pepper
2 stalks celery
1 jar of prepared pasta sauce, not tomato sauce
    (needs more spices)
1 19 oz can diced tomatoes
1 cup water
1 ½ cups pasta

What you'll do:
1. Wash your hands.
2. Wash all vegetables.
   Cut the vegetables into workable sizes.
3. If you have one, use a deep skillet; add 2 tablespoons of olive oil. Turn element on to medium high heat.
4. When oil is up to temperature, add the garlic and onions. Brown quickly. Be careful not to let them burn by leaving them in one place too long. Two minutes should be fine.
5. Add meat, peppers and celery. Brown everything. Stir frequently. Browning should take 3–4 minutes. Drain or blot fat.
6. Once browned, add the pasta sauce, diced tomatoes and the water. Then add the pasta, ensuring the pasta is completely covered by the sauce.
7. Cover and cook for 15–20 minutes.
8. Stir occasionally.

Tips

1   Give your eyes a break: instead of the usual way of cutting vegetables, cut them on a diagonal – like they do in fancy restaurants. This way, you could make the same meal two days in a row and kids will think it's a different meal.

2   If you got the Manual Chopper for a gift, drag it out, peel some garlic and give it a whirl. All meals are SO much better with fresh garlic.

3   The sizzling sound of a small piece of vegetable in the oil as it heats up will tell you when it's up to temperature.

This is a recipe my girlfriend's parents got from their grandparents on Cache Lake, Ontario, close to the Manitoba border, which was originally called Indian Corn. I feel self-conscious referring to it as such in case it insults anyone, so I'm going the PC route.

What you'll need:
1 cup Uncle Ben's rice
1 cup water
1 ½ lbs lean ground beef
1 small can of creamed corn
1 small can tomatoes
salt and pepper to taste

What you'll do:
1.   Wash your hands.
2.   Cook rice first in 1 cup water (7 minutes in the microwave, double that on the stovetop). Set aside.
3.   Cook ground beef, drain, add rice, corn, tomatoes, mix well.
4.   Cook on medium heat 15 minutes, stirring occasionally. Don't forget to salt and pepper to taste.

Tip

1   The longer these types of meals simmer, the better they taste. Bear in mind, this is definitely a meal that encourages you to add the spices you like, otherwise, it could be accused of being bland. So, don't be shy with the salt and pepper.

Burger Stroganoff

Beef Stroganoff is a classic that is covered in the **Famous Forkers** section later on, but this recipe provides most of the taste in a big hurry.

What you'll need
1 ½ teaspoons olive oil
1 medium onion, sliced thinly
1 lb of lean ground beef
¼ teaspoon garlic powder
2 cups vegetable broth
1 8 oz can mushroom stems and pieces, drained
2 ½ cups medium egg noodles
1 8 oz container sour cream

asparagus is my suggested vegetable to complement this meal

What you'll do:
1. Wash your hands.
2. Using medium-high heat, heat oil in a large deep skillet. Add onion.
3. Brown onion until crisp and lightly browned, stirring from time to time.
4. Add and brown ground beef.
5. Add everything else except for the sour cream. Mix well, bring to a boil.
6. Reduce to low heat and cover. Simmer for about 10 minutes (until noodles are tender).
7. Remove from heat. Stir in sour cream. Serve.

Hangover Corned Beef Hash

This is a great meal for dinner and, if you have leftovers after a party, would make a great breakfast, too!

What you'll need:
splotch of olive oil (a splotch, don't forget, is about the size
    of two silver dollars)
2 onions, chopped
4 potatoes, chopped (you can peel them if you want,
    but it's not necessary)
2 cans corned beef
1 tablespoon ground black pepper
1 ½ tablespoons cider vinegar
vegetable of choice

What you'll do:
1. Wash your hands.
2. Heat oil in a large skillet over medium high heat.
3. Sauté onions and potatoes until slightly browned
4. Add and brown corned beef. Mix everything together.
5. Add pepper and vinegar.
6. Reduce heat to medium-low.
7. Cover skillet and cook for 20 minutes.

Cindy's Shipwreck Casserole

This recipe is from a friend's cousin, Cindy, and since no one told me how the name came about, I found myself wondering (as we are wont to do while making a new recipe) how the name came about – it certainly wasn't created by some gooner tramping around a seemingly deserted island trying to avoid being dinner themselves. Unless it's a recipe that would best be received by someone who just got off the island after 5 years of snails and swordfish, although that seems doubtful too. Imagine if we named meals based on who in what circumstances would appreciate them most? ANYWAY.

What you'll need:
splotch of olive oil
1 lb lean ground beef
1 small onion
6 potatoes, peeled, thinly sliced
1 cup of white rice
1 tin of tomato soup
1 tin of water

What you'll do:
1. Wash your hands.
2. In a large skillet, heat a small amount of olive oil.
3. Add ground beef and onion to heated oil and brown thoroughly.
4. Drain.
5. Into a 9 x 13 casserole dish, place a thin layer of the browned ground beef.
6. Add a layer of the thinly sliced potatoes.
7. Keep layering one after the other, making sure the top layer is ground beef.
8. Pour uncooked rice over the entire casserole.
9. Pour the soup/water mixture over entire casserole.
10. Place in preheated to 350F oven and cook for 2 hours.

Baked Putanesca Heaven

This is a combo between Pasta Putanesca, Hamburger Heaven and Make it Bake it Spaghetti. The former is a hit because the Italian sausage has a nice bite to it, the latter is a hit because the vegetables and lean ground beef provide a comforting taste and the baked version offers a nice change. THIS recipe combines the bite of the sausage flavor, reassurance of the ground beef and tops it off with the baked texture. This one will be a hit if you live in a cold climate (I doubt it'll be a Florida main feature unless it's below 50F).

What you'll need:
couple splotches of olive oil
2 cloves garlic, minced or chopped
1 onion, chopped
1 mild Italian sausage (you may like Hot)
1 lb lean ground beef
1 can of diced tomatoes
1 jar of Classico Sun Dried Tomatoes
- your choice of pasta, enough for 4 people (why 4, you ask? Because we're after leftovers and a certain pasta/sauce ratio)
- grateable cheese - Cheddar, Mozzarella, whatever
- oregano or Italian multi-spice

What you'll do:
1. peel the skin off the sausage and cut into roughly 1" pieces.
2. on medium high, heat the olive oil.
3. add the garlic and onion.
4. saute until the onion is translucent.
5. add the sausage and brown.
6. add the ground beef when the sausage is halfway browned.
7. brown everything together.
8. once browned, drain off the fat then add can of tomatoes and jar of sauce, stir, and add spices.
9. cover and turn down to 1/4 heat.
10. put the pasta on.
11. heat oven to 325.
12. once pasta is cooked, drain.

13. Remove half of sauce, put into a fridgeable container
14. mix pasta and remaining sauce, and move to a casserole dish.
15. grate cheese over top
16. cover and put into oven for about 1/2 hour (longer is better but we never have the time).
17. Take the cover off with about 10 minutes remaining if you like the top of the pasta to get a little crunchy.

Murphy's Serendipitous Chicken

Murphy's Law: "If there are two or more ways to do something, and one of those ways can result in a catastrophe, then someone will do it."

Serendipity: "The faculty of making fortunate discoveries by accident."

The American Heritage® Dictionary of the English Language, Fourth Edition

I discovered this recipe by accident (hence the name), and rather than making everybody ill (a true Murphy moment), everyone loved it (a true serendipitous – I dare you to say that out loud – moment). Also, it never ceases to amaze me how impossible it is to make enough of this to have seconds; instead of the whatever-can-go-wrong-will-go-wrong Murphy's Law, apply the whatever-I-make-of-this-meal-will-get-eaten-in-one-sitting Wright's Law.

What you'll need:
1 or 2 boneless chicken breasts
1 green pepper
1 red pepper
1 stalk celery
1 clove of garlic
1 medium onion
olive oil
vegetable stock
1 cup pasta, preferably rotini

What you'll do:
1. Wash your hands.
2. Cut the chicken breasts into 1" pieces (roughly)
3. Cut the peppers and celery into thin strips
4. Peel the garlic and chop into small pieces (dig out your Manual Chopper)
5. Cut the onions into sections
6. Add 2 tablespoons olive oil to your pan, heat.
7. Add garlic and onions. Brown for a moment.

8. Sauté the chicken first but add peppers and celery after a moment (you're just giving the chicken a little head start but you want the combined taste of all three things cooking).
9. Once ingredients are cooked (check the chicken by cutting into the biggest piece and make sure it's white – no pink chicken allowed!).
10. Add a minor splash more olive oil and a cup of vegetable stock. Stir.
11. Add the pasta. Stir
12. Cover and cook for 15–20 minutes, or until you've achieved your preferred texture for pasta (less time = al dente).

If you'd rather make the pasta separate from the sauce, put a large pot of water on to boil when you start browning the chicken.

Cooking with a wok is almost a fail-safe method of cooking healthily and tastily (is there really such a word?). The reason I think woks are great, especially for us guys, is because it doesn't really matter what things are going in, they don't have to be cut uniformly for all that "presentation" stuff. The smaller the pieces, the quicker you can eat, though, so keep that in mind. Of course, if you're cooking a meal for a first date, you can make a big show about how adept you are with a sharp knife, something that impresses women with nerves of steel. This is one of my boys' and my favorite meals because it's extremely tasty, extremely quick and extremely nutritious.

What you'll need:
½ lb beef sirloin cut into strips
2 stalks of broccoli
1 large stalk of celery
1 large carrot
1 medium onion
1 each of green and red pepper
couple splotches of cooking oil
2 cups instant rice
4–6 squirts of Soya Sauce

NOTE: Your supermarket probably sells packages of beef steak that's been cut into strips for easy stir-frying. Get half a pound, or, if we shop at the same store, buy the smallest package – usually a pound, and freeze half. The beauty of the wok is you're able to use a fraction of what you think you'll need. The only spice you need, of course, is Soya sauce.

What you'll do:
1. Wash your hands.
2. Cut the beef strips into bite-size pieces.
3. Cut the vegetables into bite-size pieces: slivers for everything but the onions, which you'll cut into rings.
4. Put the element on high and add 2 tablespoons of cooking oil into the wok to heat up. I always put one piece of onion in the pan to indicate when the oil's up to heat – when it starts to sizzle, it's ready.
5. As the oil is heating up, measure the rice (equal parts rice and water – the box will tell you how much for the number of people you're feeding). Don't go too far away from the wok, as it will heat up faster than you think.
6. Once the oil is hot, add the beef and the rest of the onions.

7. When the beef is almost thoroughly browned, start the rice in a covered dish in the microwave.
8. Once the meat is browned (take a piece out and test it by cutting it in half)
9. Dump in the rest of the vegetables and STIR FRY, baby!
10. After 1 minute or so of stir-frying, add the Soya sauce.
11. Cook for 4 minutes for firm vegetables, 6 for mushier ones.

Tips

1   Stir-frying, surprisingly, means you keep "stirring" while the food is frying. You shouldn't leave stuff in one place for too long. This is not one of those meals you can wok away from, as it were. This is a stir until it's done kind of meal.

2   Don't put in so much Soya sauce or water that you're boiling everything.

3   As long as the meat is properly cooked, it doesn't really matter how long you cook the vegetables; obviously, the less time, the crunchier, the more time, the mushier.

4   Don't use olive oil with wok cooking; doesn't work well at all. Use canola or safflower – anything with a high smoking point, peanut is the favorite of many but since I'm allergic, it ain't my choice, and as my girlfriend says, it's all about me.

5   Don't be tempted into making a salad with this meal, doesn't go well.

6   What does go well is some toast from French or Italian bread.

Another Note: ... You can make 3 other meals using the wok basics: substitute chicken or pork for beef, use potatoes in stead of rice, or no meat, just vegetables with rice or potatoes.

You can use either Parmesan or Mozzarella cheese for this cheesy chicken dish. Perhaps you could use Parmesan the first few times and then switch. Hey, just trying to help.

What you'll need:
splotch of olive oil
4 skinless, boneless chicken breasts
½ teaspoon ground black pepper
½ teaspoon minced garlic
¼ cup minced onion
½ cup vegetable broth
4 cups spaghetti sauce
1 cup shredded Mozzarella or Parmesan cheese

What you'll do:
1. Wash your hands.
2. Heat oil in a large skillet over ¾ (medium high) heat.
3. Sauté chicken breasts for 4 to 5 minutes each side, or until white on the outside.
4. Add pepper, garlic, onion and broth.
5. Cover and simmer over medium heat until broth cooks off, about 7 to 10 minutes.
6. Stir in spaghetti sauce, then cover and simmer another 10 minutes, or until chicken is cooked through and no longer pink inside.
7. Sprinkle cheese on top, cover and cook for another 2 to 3 minutes, or until cheese is melted.

Pie-Free Chicken Pot Pie

This meal has the taste and comfort of a pot pie but without the pie.

What you'll need:
Small splotch olive oil
1 medium onion, chopped
3 skinless, boneless chicken breasts
1 12 oz package egg noodles, cooked
2 12 oz jars chicken gravy
2 cups frozen green peas, thawed

What you'll do:
1. Wash your hands.
2. Heat oil in large skillet.
3. Put water on for pasta and cook when water's ready.
4. Sauté onion until translucent.
5. Cut chicken into bite-size pieces and brown. Make sure chicken is cooked.
6. Add cooked, drained and still hot noodles to chicken in skillet and pour in gravy and frozen peas.
7. Stir together until ingredients are well mixed.
8. Reduce heat to medium low, cover, and simmer for 10 minutes.

Baggie's Pork Stew

Baggie, by the way, is not some distant Scottish relative who gave me this recipe. No, that would make too much sense. Baggie refers to a baguette, the perfect piece of bread to harness this stew.

What you'll need:

2 tablespoons olive oil
2 tablespoons flour
1 ½ pounds trimmed pork tenderloin, cut into 1-inch cubes
1 large onion, chopped
1 cup thickly sliced small mushrooms
4 garlic cloves, minced
½ cup dry white wine (½ a cup for me, ½ a cup for the stew,
    ½ a cup for me ...)
2 cups vegetable broth
2 tablespoons tomato paste
1 ½ teaspoons dried sage
1/8 teaspoon allspice
3 tablespoons fresh parsley, minced
to taste salt and pepper
1 cup egg noodles

What you'll do:

1. Wash your hands.
2. In an oven-safe pan or Dutch oven, add 1 tablespoon oil and heat over medium-high heat.
3. Put flour into small mixing bowl.
4. Cut pork tenderloin into cubes and place in bowl holding flour. Coat pork cubes with flour by tossing (in the bowl, not around the room).
5. Once coated, place meat into pan and brown on all sides.
6. Once browned, remove to a plate. (If you're going to dawdle making this recipe, as in, take 15 minutes to watch TV in the middle of it or take an important phone call, make sure you keep the browned meat either above 150ºF or below 41ºF, for bacteria reasons. Of course you aren't going to put things you're about to use within a couple of minutes in the fridge, but it's a good habit to get into if you're frequently leaving browned

meat for more than a couple of minutes – why, I don't want to know).

7. Add remaining oil to the pan.
8. Sauté onions, mushrooms and garlic until onions are tender.
9. Add wine, chicken vegetable broth and tomato paste; stir, cooking until meat remnants have been scraped from pan bottom.
10. Stir in the sage, allspice and the set-aside meat.
11. Simmer until the meat is no longer pink, about 10 minutes.
12. Stir the parsley and season with salt and pepper.
13. Add a cup of egg noodles and cover for 10 minutes, or if you wish, make the pasta in another pot – but then, you're right, it wouldn't be a one pot meal.

Makes 4 servings or enough for 2 if one is a 15-year-old.

Pork Chop Stew

You've been waiting to braise something, I know. You can have a bit of fun with this the next day: mention to your office friends, "You should have seen the braising we did last night." Let's make a deal: I think less than 25% of the people who hear that will know what you meant, so I'll send you a buck if everyone says, "Who cares if you first browned a piece of meat in oil and then cooked it slowly in liquid?" But you owe me a buck if no one knows what the hell you're talking about. Deal? Come on! All right, forget it.

What you'll need:
2 tablespoons olive oil
3–4 pork chops
1 10¾ oz can condensed tomato soup
½ cup vegetable broth
1 teaspoon Worcestershire sauce
½ teaspoon salt
3 potatoes, quartered
4 small carrots, cut into 2 inch pieces

What you'll do:
1. Wash your hands.
2. In a large skillet, heat oil.
3. Brown pork chops over medium heat for about 4 to 6 minutes each side. Pour off fat.
4. Add the tomato soup, vegetable broth, Worcestershire sauce, salt, potatoes, and carrots.
5. Cover skillet, reduce heat to medium low and simmer for 45 minutes.

Tuna Casserole

It's unbelievable how good this meal is and how simple it is to make. It's so simple, I can't believe how long it took me to figure it out. My mother had to give me the recipe so many times, she finally got mad at me. Tuna Casserole is one of those meals Moms have made so many times they can't explain the recipe. Mind you, my mother's at the age where people get annoyed when asked questions – let alone about cooking – so it's probably a good thing I wrote it down this time.

What you'll need:

pasta	(bowtie, shell, elbow – something small)
tuna	(buy the flaked or chunk white tuna, don't get sucked into buying the light tuna because you think it has less fat, it really has less goodness; it's kind of like the hotdog or sausage of tuna)
peas	½ cup frozen peas
can	cream of broccoli soup
cheese	grateable cheese, usually cheddar
topping	Some people put crumbled chips, crackers or even bread crumbs on top (but, then again, some people are odd)

What you'll do:

1. Wash your hands.
2. First cook the pasta.
3. Drain it, then put it into an oven dish that's big enough to hold however much pasta you have to cook for the number of people you're cooking for.
4. Then mix in a can of tuna, throw in the frozen peas, pour in the can of soup, add the cheese on top and whatever you've chosen to finish off with – ground chips (crumbled in your hand, it doesn't have to be some sort of complicated, intricate grinding process).
5. Put it into a preheated oven at 325F for 25 to 30 minutes.

Weekday Whackers:
Whack it together in a hurry

These may not be one-pot wonders, but they can be whacked together in significant haste and, again, without compromising taste. My aim with this section and the previous one is to find meals that are terrifically comforting, great tasting and avoid the necessity of relying on fast foods or the frozen concoctions that contain who knows what. A number of these meals have proteins that can be easily exchanged – as can the broccoli in Broccoli Bonanza become cauliflower in the as yet un-created Cauliflower Casserole – be the first on your block to make this dish!

Beef	Spaghetti: Make it. Bake it.
	Meat Loaf
	Beef Stew
	Wok This Way
Chicken	Deep Dish Chicken Pot Pie
	Sitting Solo
	Curry Chicken Casserole
Fish	Felini Fish Filets
	Cape Breton Salmon
	Broccoli and Salmon Casserole
Vegetarian	Broccoli Bonanza

Making spaghetti and sauce is no longer a real accomplishment because of the amount of prepared sauces on the market now. But this recipe will be one you can easily make from scratch, that you could choose to have as a conventional spaghetti and sauce meal – you know, make the sauce, make the pasta, put the pasta in a bowl, add some sauce. Or you can do what I'm proposing: mix the pasta with the sauce, top it with some grated cheese and chuck it into the oven. Baked Spaghetti will become your favorite mid-Winter comfort meal!

What you'll need:
1 medium onion, chopped
1 stalk celery, sliced thinly
1 green pepper, chopped
1 red pepper, chopped
1 clove of garlic
small splotch of olive oil
1 lb lean ground beef
1 jar of pasta sauce (in case you're asking,
    the Sundried Tomato one is good)
oregano, basil and pepper to taste
handful of grated cheese of choice (mozzarella, parmesan)

What you'll do:
1. Wash your hands.
2. Wash the vegetables.
3. Cut them into workable sizes.
4. Chop garlic (if you have the time and the tools).
5. Heat up olive oil in skillet on medium-high heat and pre-heat oven to 325.
6. Give the vegetables a little (1 minute) head start in the skillet before adding the meat.
7. Add meat. Brown everything thoroughly. (Most recipes recommend draining off the oil, for obvious reasons. Sometimes I do, sometimes I don't. It tastes better when you don't. Unless you're using extra lean ground beef, it's probably better if you do.)

8. Add pasta sauce and spices.
9. Cover. Turn down heat to low heat and simmer for 20 minutes.
10. Cook pasta while this is simmering.
11. When pasta is cooked (about 20 minutes), combine sauce and pasta in a casserole dish, sprinkle grated cheese (mozzarella/parmesan) on top, and place in oven for 20 minutes covered and then 10 without cover.

Meat Loaf

When I was growing up and my brother (who's 9 years older than me) lived away from home, I used to know when he was expected for dinner because my mother would make his favorite meal – meat loaf. Honestly. I thought I had a one of those clairvoyant gifts, but it was really only an unrealized recognition of a) how good my mother's meat loaf was and b) how predictable my brother was. Incidentally, I'm still not sure if he makes his own meat loaf, so Rick, here's the recipe!

What you'll need:
½ cup packed brown sugar
½ cup ketchup
1 ½ lbs lean ground beef
¾ cup milk
2 eggs
1 ½ teaspoons salt
¼ teaspoon ground black pepper
1 small onion, chopped
¾ cup bread crumbs

What you'll do:
1. Wash your hands.
2. Preheat oven to 350 degrees F (175 degrees C). Lightly grease a 5x9 inch loaf pan.
3. Press the brown sugar in the bottom of the prepared loaf pan and spread ½ the ketchup over the sugar.
4. In a mixing bowl, mix thoroughly all remaining ingredients, shape into a loaf and place into the loaf pan. Place remaining ketchup on top of loaf.
5. Bake in preheated oven for 1 hour, until the internal temp is 165F or until juices are clear.

Beef Stew

This wouldn't generally be considered a Weekday Whacker because stews take around 3 hours, but if you have a pressure cooker it can be ready in about an hour. And don't forget, because you're making a stew, don't be too concerned about whether everything's precision-cut.

What you'll need:
1 ½ lbs beef, chuck or round
3 leeks
2 carrots
1 large potato
1 onion
1 turnip
1 rib (stalk) celery
olive oil
1 ½ cups water
1 cup beef broth (or tin of consommé)
½ cup red wine
salt and pepper to taste

What you'll do:
1. Wash your hands.
2. Cut the beef into 1" pieces –unless you find a package of stewing beef.
3. Thinly slice the 3 leeks.
4. Peel the carrots, halve them lengthwise and cut into 1" pieces.
5. Wash, peel and cut into bite-size pieces the potato
6. Peel the onion and slice them into sections.
7. Peel the turnip and chop it coarsely, which means, in case you're wondering (as I did), that you don't have to cut it uniformly.
8. Slice the celery rib into 1" pieces.
9. Add 2 or 3 tablespoons of olive oil (a splash) to pressure cooker and bring up to heat on medium-high.
10. Once hot, add beef and brown.
11. Remove the meat leaving the residual oil and pan drippings.
12. Add the vegetables to cooker. Sauté vegetables until lightly browned, (almost 5 minutes of fairly constant stirring).

13. Add the browned beef, the liquid and salt/pepper to taste.
14. Cover, lock and bring to full steam. Cook for 40 minutes.
15. Remove from heat. Release steam quickly.

Tips

1   If you're new to a pressure cooker, monitor how much steam is coming out. The optimum level of steam is what's generated at a little hotter than medium heat. If you use maximum heat, you'll just run out of liquid.

2   For cleaning leeks, peel a couple of layers off until you get to a level that doesn't have dirt, then wash.

3   Peeling turnips is a lot like peeling a candle – very slippery. The easiest way is to not try to "peel" it, rather, slice off the waxy cover. If you have a microwave oven, try putting the turnip in it on high for a couple of minutes to soften it up.

Once you've mastered the wok (or at least cooked the simple meals in it often enough to become more adventurous), here's a meal you can make during the week that's tasty beyond belief.

What you'll need for the sauce:
1 teaspoon cornstarch
1 teaspoon sugar
1 tablespoon beef stock
1 teaspoon orange peel, finely shredded
¾ cup orange juice
1 tablespoon soya sauce

What you'll need for the main ingredients:
½ lb beef top round steak, cut into strips
1 tablespoon cooking oil (canola)
1 garlic clove, minced
4 green onions, sliced into 1" pieces
2 large broccoli heads, cut into bite-size pieces
2 cups cooked white rice (hot)

What you'll do for the sauce:
In a measuring cup, combine all of the sauce ingredients and set aside.

What you'll do for the main:
1. Wash your hands.
2. Wash the vegetables and cut.
3. Beef: slice thinly across the grain into strips.
4. Over medium-high heat, add a little canola oil to wok and bring up to heat.
5. Stir-fry garlic and onion 1 minute and remove from wok.
6. Stir-fry half of the beef for 2 to 3 minutes.
7. Remove form the wok and stir-fry the rest of the beef.
8. Return all of the beef to the wok.
9. Stir in the sauce.
10. Cook and stir until bubbly (about 1 minute).
11. Stir in uncooked broccoli and onion mixture.
12. Cover and cook for 1 minute.

Serve over rice.

Deep Dish Chicken Pot Pie

I know you're going to ask, "Why am I going to all this trouble if I can just go and buy a chicken pot pie?" It's a fair question, but you have to make this first. The one thing I like about this recipe, aside from the fact it TASTES homemade, is that whenever I eat one of the frozen pot pies, I'm always pretty sure they don't have the same chicken-choosing criteria I have.

What you'll need:
1 15 oz package refrigerated pie crusts
   (they come in a package of 2)
¼ cup butter or margarine
½ cup chopped onion
1/3 cup all-purpose flour
½ cup of chicken stock (in a measuring cup, add a tablespoon
   of powdered stock to hot water)
½ tsp thyme
1/8 teaspoon ground black pepper
1 ½ cups water
¾ cup milk
2 cups frozen mixed vegetables, thawed
2 ½ cups diced cooked chicken
2 teaspoons of diced pimento (they come in small jars,
   ask your grocer)

What you'll do:
1. Wash your hands.
2. Heat oven to 400 degrees F.
3. Place one pie crust into a 10" deep pie plate.
4. In large saucepan over medium heat, add butter and bring up to temperature.
5. Add onion and sauté until tender. Stir in flour, stock, thyme and pepper.
6. Add water and milk all at once. Cook and stir until thickened and bubbly. Stir in mixed vegetables, chicken, and pimento.
7. Pour mixture into crust in pie plate.

8. Place remaining crust on top to cover chicken mixture. Flute* edges of pastry and cut slits in the top to allow the steam to escape.
9. Bake for 25–30 minutes or until pastry is golden brown and filling is hot.

* Flute means to make ruffles, as in, make the edges imitate an Irish rolling hill landscape by pressing down with your thumb around the entire pie. You don't have to do this for any cooking or structural reason; it just makes it look better.

Sitting Solo

Sometimes you've just gotta treat yourself right. This is a great meal if you're only cooking for yourself but feel like a bit of solo pampering.

What you'll need:
½ cup butter
2 skinless, boneless chicken breasts
¼ cup lemon juice
¼ cup grated Parmesan cheese

What you'll do:
1. Wash your hands.
2. In a medium skillet over medium-high heat, melt 2 tablespoons of the butter.
3. Once up to heat, add chicken to skillet and cook, about 5 to 7 minutes.
4. When chicken is browned, add remaining butter and the lemon juice.
5. Sauté for 7 minutes, then remove chicken from skillet. Cover to keep warm.
6. Add cheese to skillet, stir with the butter and lemon juice until mixture has become a sauce, then pour the sauce over the chicken.

This meal is great with asparagus and some scalloped potatoes, plain pasta or white rice. It's a little rich to have with a flavored rice, in my opinion.

I really like this meal, but you kind of have to like curry to like this dish. If you don't like curry, this is a meal you'd best avoid, or you could do as one of my Cooking for the Domestically Challenged students did: just tear the page out of the book (would that be an "imbalanced" approach to meal planning??). Done properly, this dinner is great; just keep an eye on how much curry you put in.

What you'll need:
1 can cream of chicken/asparagus/broccoli soup
    (the / means it's your choice!) mixed with ½ can of water
1 cup mayonnaise
1 teaspoon curry powder
½ can of milk
2 large heads of broccoli, chopped
2 tablespoons olive oil
5 chicken breasts or 2 cups leftover chicken
mucho ground pepper
¾ cup grated cheddar cheese
½ cup bread crumbs

What you'll do:
1. Wash your hands.
2. In a small mixing bowl, combine soup mixture, mayonnaise, curry powder and 2 tablespoons water. Be sure everything is mixed until smooth.
3. Preheat oven to 375F.
4. In a medium fry pan, bring olive oil up to temperature over medium heat.
5. Fry chicken until well cooked, generously adding ground pepper as you fry.
6. Once cooked, cut chicken into cubes.
7. Place broccoli into ungreased casserole dish.
8. Place chicken chunks over broccoli.
9. Spread the soup mixture (give it a final stir before spreading) over the chicken.
10. Sprinkle cheese over the whole GD thing.
11. Sprinkle breadcrumbs over top of cheese.
12. Bake uncovered for 45 minutes.

Felini Fish Filet

Here's your chance to braise fish! Try cod and haddock fillets for a change.

What you'll need:
2 tablespoons olive oil
1 onion, thinly sliced
2 cloves garlic, minced
1 14-½ oz can diced tomatoes
1 tablespoon chopped fresh parsley
½ cup dry white wine
1 pound cod or haddock fillets

What you'll do:
Wash your hands.
1. In a large frying pan, heat oil over medium heat.
2. Sauté onions and garlic in olive oil for about 2 minutes – until softened.
3. Stir in tomatoes, parsley, and wine. Reduce heat to low and simmer for 5 minutes.
4. Place fillets in sauce. Simmer for about 5 more minutes, or until fish turns white.

When I was doing media interviews to promote my book Cook Like a Mother!, I visited the East Coast. While flying there, I sat next to a woman who lived with her husband and family in Cape Breton. I mentioned what I was doing and expressed a desire to make a recipe during my interview that would reflect a local touch. Here's what she suggested and what has become a favorite with my boys and me.

What you'll need:
aluminum foil
butter or olive oil
1 filet of salmon (explain to fish seller the number of people
    you're serving to determine size)
3–4 green onions, chopped
bread crumbs (enough to cover size of fish you're cooking)
lemon pepper (to taste)
roast garlic spice (or garlic/parsley salt)
rosemary

What you'll do:

1. Wash your hands.
2. Take about 18" of aluminum foil.
3. Make a spot for olive oil (curve up foil so olive oil stays put – not necessary of course, if you use butter).
4. Place salmon skin down.
5. Add chopped green onions.
6. Sprinkle breadcrumbs to lightly cover fish.
7. Add spices.
8. Wrap.
9. Put on BBQ grill for 12–15 minutes on medium heat for a medium-size salmon (the rule of thumb is about 10 minutes per inch of fish).

Note: If you're a seafood lover, add 3 scallops and then crabmeat before adding green onions, breadcrumbs and spices.

Broccoli and Salmon Casserole

If you like broccoli and love salmon, this is the dish for you! If you don't, turn the page!

What you'll need:
3 cups frozen chopped broccoli flowers
small splash of olive oil
¼ cup chopped onion
2 tablespoons all-purpose flour
1 ½ cups milk
¾ cup grated mozzarella cheese
½ cup chopped mushrooms (you can use canned mushrooms)
1 tablespoon chopped parsley
1 small tin of shredded pink salmon
¼ cup Parmesan cheese

What you'll do:
1. Wash your hands.
2. Preheat your oven to 350 degrees F.
3. Steam broccoli until just tender.
4. Heat the olive oil in a large skillet and sauté the onion until soft and translucent.
5. Remove the onion using a slotted spoon.
6. Stir the flour into the remaining oil in the skillet; when the mixture bubbles add the milk and stir constantly to keep lumps from forming.
7. Add the mozzarella cheese, mushrooms and parsley; stir until the cheese has melted.
8. Add the salmon, steamed broccoli and onions.
9. Spray 2-quart casserole dish with Pam.
10. Stir mixture then transfer to the casserole dish.
11. Sprinkle the Parmesan cheese over the top and bake uncovered for 35 minutes or until the Parmesan is lightly browned.

A great side dish would be Lipton SideKicks Scalloped Potatoes, which you could bake in the oven next to the casserole.

OK, so I'm a self-proclaimed broccoli poster-gooner, so what? You can certainly replace the broccoli with cauliflower, then it becomes Cauliflower Casserole – but broccoli's the best!

What you'll need:
2 large stalks of fresh broccoli, chopped
1 16 oz package rotini or penne pasta
½ cup olive oil
2 cloves garlic, minced
½ cup grated Parmesan cheese
salt and ground black pepper to taste

What you'll do:
1. Wash your hands.
2. In a large pot, cook broccoli in boiling water until tender – don't overcook!
3. Drain broccoli, put aside and reserve cooking water.
4. Cook pasta in reserved broccoli cooking water.
5. Drain and put aside pasta.
6. Add olive oil to the pot, heat and sauté the garlic for a couple of minutes.
7. Add the cooked pasta, broccoli, grated Parmesan cheese and toss together. If desired, add salt and pepper to taste.

Famous Forkers:
Recognizable Repasts

Most of us have favorite or special meals we've had somewhere along the way. Maybe it was your Mom, your boyfriend's Mom or your favorite restaurant that created a tasty meal you associate with a special occasion. My brother's favorite meal was meat loaf, mine was lasagna, my sister's was Shepherd's Pie. In our early, formative years, these meals represented great culinary skill, but in reality, they were probably far easier to make than you realize.

This chapter will deal with how to make these defining meals, which are probably best kept for the weekend or holidays, mainly because you need to spend a touch more time preparing them.

Yer Traditional Roast Chicken
Chicken Cacciatore
R V Chicken
Marinated Lemon Chicken
Chicken Parmesan
Grilled Salmon
Some Sort of Cranberry Port Roast
Pork Roast Thyme
Roast Beef
Beef Pot Roast
Hey, Foil This Pot Roast
Saturday Night Beef
Shepherd's Pie
Lasagna
Beef Stroganoff
Veal Marsala
Roman Conqueror Casserole
Pasta Putanesca
Risotto
Ratatouille

Yer Traditional Roast Chicken

For the longest time, my stovetop was an only child. I knew it was related, closely, in fact, to the oven, but I just wasn't comfortable making friends with this almost out-of-reach, difficult-to-understand acquaintance. But, recently I decided the worst thing my oven could do was wreck my dinner and burn down my house, so I decided to use it more frequently. Once you get over a common apprehension about using an oven (maybe it's just me), you can make some terrific meals. One of them that works really well as a testing ground for cooking a Christmas turkey is a small roast chicken.

What you'll need:
3 lb chicken
olive oil
garlic salt
pepper
oregano
2 broccoli stalks
2 cups of instant rice
salt, pepper, oregano

What you'll do:
1. Wash your hands.
2. Clean the chicken by running it under cold or warm water and gently scrubbing, making sure you've removed the giblet (look inside the cavity).
3. Preheat the oven to 325F.
4. Put the chicken into a roasting pan, breast facing up (the same way it looked when you bought it).
5. Using a brush, lightly coat the chicken with olive oil which makes the skin turn a nicer shade of brown and makes it taste better.
6. Sprinkle garlic salt, pepper, oregano and paprika if you have some. Not too much, just enough to make it look like you've added some spices.
7. Cook the bird for 25 minutes a pound.

8. Set the timer to go off about 10 minutes early so you can put the instant rice in the microwave to cook.
9. Halfway through the rice cooking, start steaming the broccoli, which will take no more than 5 minutes.

Tip

1   Use a fresh chicken. If you think trying to extract the bag of giblets from a fresh chicken is tricky, wait until you try to get a grip on a semi-frozen bag and pull it out without tearing it. Having to worry about whether the bird has been properly thawed isn't worth the small savings it offers.

Chicken Cacciatore

There's some sort of unwritten rule that girls have to serve this to their boyfriend as their first meal together – or, for that matter, that boyfriends serve it to their girlfriends – just to demonstrate how well-versed they are in the kitchen, so here's an ode to Teen Love.

What you'll need:
1 tablespoon olive oil
1/3 cup chopped onion
1 clove garlic, chopped
1/3 cup chopped green pepper
¾ lb chicken meat, cooked and cubed
1 small can of whole peeled tomatoes
½ cup green beans
¼ teaspoon dried oregano

What you'll do:
1. Wash your hands.
2. In a large skillet over medium-high heat, heat olive oil.
3. Once hot, sauté onion, garlic and green pepper until soft.
4. Add chicken and brown.
5. Add tomatoes, beans and oregano. Stir well.
6. Lower heat to medium-low.
7. Simmer for 8 to 10 minutes, stirring non-stop.
8. Remove from heat and serve hot.

This could indeed be chicken you can cook while traveling across the country in your RV, but it really refers to Raspberry Vinegar (if you don't have raspberry vinegar lying around, what about balsamic – do you have some of that? Well, then, use it!). By the way, I know the steps seem onerous because there are so many of them, but I'm trying to help you stumble through this process without anything derailing it, so if the steps sometimes seem a little simplistic, I can assure you they're worthwhile.

What you'll need:
1 cup all-purpose flour
1 ½ lbs of boneless, skinless chicken breasts
3 tablespoons olive oil
ground pepper
salt
½ teaspoon oregano
1/3 cup of raspberry vinegar
½ cup of snow peas (handful)
1 lb cherry tomatoes

What you'll do:
1. Wash your hands.
2. Cut chicken into 2" pieces.
3. Preheat oven to 220F.
4. Put the cup of flour in a strainer/sieve and hold it over a bowl. Add the chicken pieces to the flour and shake to coat the chicken, letting the flour fall through to the bowl. BE SURE TO THROW OUT THE LEFTOVER FLOUR!
5. In a large skillet, heat half the oil over medium-high heat.
6. Once up to temperature, add the chicken pieces and sauté, stirring frequently until cooked. (NOTE: if recipes ever ask you to cook meat in two batches, it's because sometimes cooking a large amount of meat can cause so much liquid to be released, it changes the method of cooking from sautéing to boiling. So, if you realize you have so much meat you can't see the bottom of the pan, do it in two batches.)

7. While cooking, season with ground pepper, salt and oregano.
8. Once cooked (no longer pink in the middle of the biggest piece), remove to a platter and either cover with aluminum foil or put in the oven to keep warm.
9. Add vinegar and cook until you've reduced (look this term up in **Stuff You Should Know** if you've forgotten!) it to a couple of tablespoons (this will take about 5 minutes).
11. Take the chicken out of the oven and pour this sauce over it.
12. Return platter of chicken to oven.
13. In the skillet that you've returned to the heat, add the remaining oil.
14. Add the snow peas and cook for 2 minutes.
15. Add the cherry tomatoes and cook for 1 minute. Season with salt and pepper while cooking.

Guys' serving version ... Yank the chicken out of the oven, slap the vegetables around the chicken and throw it on the table (I hope you have a touch more panache than I do).

Gals' serving version ... Retrieve the chicken from the oven, place the vegetables around the chicken in an aesthetically pleasing design and place it with a flourish on the table.

Marinated Lemon Chicken

This is a meal that's easy to make and is more visually impressive than most meals. As we know, there are times you'd like to have something that not only tastes good, but looks good, too. You don't have to be a gourmet cook to make something visually appealing. This is the sort of meal you'd serve if you were having another couple for dinner and you've had pasta three nights in a row, made roast beef for them last time and had pot roast in your pressure cooker the time before that. The only caveat to this recipe is that you need to do Steps 1 to 7 no less than 2 hours before dinner (for the marinade to marinate).

What you'll need:

6 boneless chicken breasts (1 per person and maybe a couple
    extra for lunch tomorrow or if someone really wants more)
olive oil
2 cloves of garlic
1 lemon (the yellow thing you get in the produce section –
    not your best friend's car)
1 of those plastic lemon-shaped juice things
generous sprinkle of oregano
1 each green, red and yellow peppers
3 cups instant rice
Keep in mind that the longer you can keep meat marinating, the more flavorful, so try to do the marinating portion (points 2 to 7 below) a few hours before your guests come over for dinner.

What you'll do:

1. Wash your hands.
2. Put the chicken in a container that is big enough to hold 6 breasts flat.
3. Pour about ½ an inch of olive oil into the bottom of the container over the chicken.
4. Finely chop or crush the garlic cloves and sprinkle all over the chicken.
5. Cut the lemon in half and using a fork, grind out the juice over the chicken allowing the occasional piece of lemon (doesn't matter if some seeds are included – it's just a marinade) to fall onto the chicken.

6. Pour a little of the lemon juice from the container (couple of squirts here and there – where you think you missed with the real lemon) over the chicken.

7. Sprinkle the chicken with the oregano, trying to be even with your sprinkling.

8. Cover the container with plastic wrap and place in the fridge until you're ready to cook the chicken.

9. Wash the peppers and slice into big, thick strips, thicker than you'd do for sauces, so they won't fall through the grill on your BBQ.

10. Measure enough rice for the number of people you're having (follow the measurements on the box – it's usually equal parts rice and water). Measure the water but don't put it in.

11. Put the chicken on the barbecue to cook first, for about 20 minutes.

12. When the chicken is nearly all cooked, grill the peppers for 2 minutes.

13. Try to time putting your peppers on the grill so they're ready when the chicken is (don't get hung up about it, check the internal temperature of the chicken: 170F).

14. Go into the house, add the water to the rice and put it in the microwave for approximately 7 minutes. Do this quickly because peppers can burn in minutes.

15. When the peppers and chicken have finished cooking, remove from the BBQ and take inside.

Tip

1   If you sliced the peppers too thinly and they seem like they're going to fall through the grill, take the grate from your toaster oven out and put it sideways on the BBQ grill. Or, you can always ask for one of those nifty grill-top vegetable thingies for a gift.

Chicken Parmesan

Here's a little story for you, just in case you need any further incentive to get a meat thermometer. In a recent class, I held a draw for the students to win a chance to learn how to make their favorite meal, and this was the winning recipe. The author of the recipe, the student's mother, listed the total cooking time as 20–25 minutes, which as you know from the chapter Stuff You Should Know, is the minutes per pound chicken takes to cook. So, I pulled it out of the oven after the allotted time and of course, it was pinker than a Barbie doll's bikini. Back into the oven it went, periodically being checked with my meat thermometer to gauge its doneness. It took about an hour to cook and if we hadn't had a meat thermometer, it would have been a bummer – literally. So, my point is, it doesn't really matter when you think something should be ready, make sure it is ready.

This a meal you can make a thousand times because it's so good. It's also a meal that's easy to make for a group of friends that won't take too long to put together – you can even do the preparations while they're telling you what they did on their summer holidays, and God knows you could use a diversion during that endless story. Serves 4

What you'll need:
1 cup Parmesan cheese
¾ cup breadcrumbs
1 teaspoon oregano
½ teaspoon pepper
½ teaspoon garlic powder
1 cup salted butter or non-hydrogenated margarine
4 boneless, skinless chicken breasts, cut into quarters

What you'll do:
1. Wash your hands.
2. Preheat oven to 350 degrees F.
3. Combine all dry ingredients in a bowl.
4. Melt butter and pour into a different bowl.
5. Dip each piece of chicken in butter, letting excess drip off before dipping in dry mixture.

6. Once coated, place chicken in a 9" x 12" casserole dish. Make sure chicken ends up in single layer, even if smushed tightly.
7. Cover (with aluminum foil if you don't have proper cover), place in the oven and cook for an hour. Because cooking time can be influenced by number of pieces of chicken, be sure to verify doneness with meat thermometer: internal temp should be 170 degrees F.

Grilled Salmon Steak

You could either grill this on a BBQ if you have one, an indoor grill if you don't, or in the oven if you don't have either of these. As a health note, experts suggest eating fish that's high in Omega 3 Fatty Acids (sounds bad but actually is very good) twice a week. Fish that rank well are salmon and tuna, so, salmon once a week and a tuna sandwich will do it.

What you'll need:
2 stalks of broccoli
potato (1 per person)
salmon steaks (one per person), 1" or less in thickness
olive oil
lemon pepper

What you'll do:
1. Wash your hands.
2. Wash the broccoli and cut into 2" pieces. Wash the potatoes.
3. Use the microwave for cooking the potatoes if you're in a hurry, otherwise put them in the oven (or toaster oven if you have one) for about 45 minutes. Potatoes are ready when you can easily pierce them with a fork. Be sure to start them way before you even think about starting your salmon.
4. Lightly brush the salmon steaks with olive oil to prevent them from drying out too much.
5. When the potatoes are about 10 minutes away from being ready (if you're using the oven), start the BBQ and heat up to medium.
6. Once you know you can devote 10 minutes or so to the salmon, put the steaks on the grill. They're too expensive to leave alone for a few minutes and get wrecked if a flame flares up. Hang with them while they cook on one side for about 5 minutes.
7. When you turn them over, dash inside and put the potatoes in the microwave for 7 minutes, if that's what you're doing with them.
8. Turn the element on under the broccoli to medium-high.
9. Dash back outside, continue cooking the salmon for another 5 minutes.
10. Take the steaks off the grill.

11. Open the potatoes, put some butter on each one and serve the works.

Note: If you can smell the fish 10 yards from the counter, take a pass and have something else. Fresh fish, contrary to what people think, doesn't smell. Do your own little test: buy some at a fresh fish market and take a whiff. Probably doesn't smell too much, right? Wait a couple of days and take a whiff of the same fish that's been in your fridge – you won't get it too close to your nose, I can assure you.

Tip

1   Do the vegetable and potato preparation before you put the salmon steaks on; they're so expensive you don't want to leave them unattended in case they get burnt or overdone.

Some Sort of Cranberry Pork Roast

When someone asks you what you're making for dinner, you have the option of saying something creative, like, "We're having a little something I call Alaskan Holiday." When they ask what the hell that is, you can reply, "Some sort of Cranberry Pork Roast." This should be the end of the questioning, because very few people have the nerve to ask two consecutive questions about what you're cooking. There's something unbelievably comforting about a roast, especially one that makes your home smell like it did on Sunday's growing up – great!

What you'll need:
1 2-½ lb boneless rolled pork loin roast
1 16 oz can jellied cranberry sauce
½ cup sugar
½ cup cranberry juice
1 teaspoon dry mustard
2 tablespoons cornstarch
2 tablespoons cold water
salt to taste

What you'll do:
Wash your hands.
1. Preheat oven to 350F.
2. Place pork roast in a roasting pan.
3. In a medium bowl, mash cranberry sauce; stir in sugar, cranberry juice, and mustard. Pour over roast. Cover and place in oven for 2 ½ hours. Check temperature every hour. You want it to reach an internal temperature of 160F.
4. Once cooked, turn off oven, remove roast and return to oven to keep it warm.
5. Time to make the gravy: Skim fat from juices; measure 2 cups of what's remaining, adding water if necessary, and pour into a saucepan. Bring to a boil over medium-high heat.
6. In a bowl, combine the cornstarch and cold water to make a paste;
7. Stir into gravy. Cook and stir until thickened. Season with salt. Serve with sliced pork.

You would have to go a long way out of your way to find a better side dish than scalloped potatoes, but that might be just me. Asparagus or broccoli (something green and crunchy) would go well with this, too.

So, everyone's tired of pot roasts, roast beef, pasta, fish, shepherd's pie, tuna casserole, beef stew, anything barbecued, etc., etc., etc.? Well, then, it's Pork Roast Thyme. This is so tasty and different, you'll be back to the well-trodden cooking ground in no thyme.

What you'll need:
5 lb pork roast, fat trimmed
3 cloves garlic, sliced
1 teaspoon salt
1 ½ teaspoons ground black pepper
3 bay leaves
½ cup cider vinegar
1 teaspoon dried thyme

What you'll do:
1. Wash your hands.
2. Preheat oven to 325 degrees F.
3. With a small knife, pierce top of roast several times. Force garlic slices into the cuts.
4. Sprinkle the roast with salt and pepper.
5. Place bay leaves in the bottom of the roasting pan, and set roast on top of bay leaves, fat side up.
6. Mix vinegar and thyme in a small bowl, and pour over the top of the roast.
7. Bake in preheated oven 3 hours, or until an internal temperature of 160 degrees F is reached.
8. Using a baster or spoon, baste the drippings over the roast frequently while it's cooking.
9. When done, let the roast cool for 10 minutes before slicing.

Tip

1   The "fat side up" refers to the fact that most roasts come with a great slab of fat attached with string to one side. If your roast doesn't have it, then, of course, if doesn't matter. Next time you buy a roast and it's missing, ask the butcher person to add a slab – really improves the taste.

Roast Beef

Very few things can more completely elicit a sense of home than a roast beef dinner. Very few things can elicit such a sense of accomplishment and peace than doing it for yourself (and a few friends, unless you are extremely hungry).

What you need:
2 stalks of fresh broccoli
4 carrots
4 potatoes
4 lb roast (rump, sirloin tip or prime rib, if you've just received a raise or a portion of your inheritance)
salt and pepper
garlic powder

What you'll do:
1. Wash your hands.
2. Wash the broccoli and cut into 2 inch pieces.
3. Peel the carrots and cut into 2 inch pieces.
4. Wash and peel the potatoes.
5. Put the roast into the roasting pan. Season with salt, pepper, garlic powder.
6. Place it in the oven, preheated to 350F.
7. Cook for 30 minutes a pound. Use a meat thermometer to gauge the level of doneness. You want the internal temperature to be around 160F.
8. Bake the washed, unpeeled potatoes. You could do put them around the roast with about an hour remaining or on the oven racks near the pan.

Tip

1   Gravy. Some people like to do interesting things for gravy with the juices in the bottom of the roasting pan. See the chapter Sides and Sauces for what to do.

You have to have had Roast Beef before you can really appreciate a Pot Roast. Why? Because let's assume you like the taste of beef. Let's assume you've enjoyed using a knife to cut some exquisitely cooked meat. Now, let's assume for a moment you want the taste of roast beef but there are two pressing concerns: one, your meat budget is a little thin and two, you want something different but still comforting. So, have you had a pot roast yet? Have you ever had beef that you don't need a knife to cut, meat that slices so easily it could be butter? And have you tasted this melt-in-your-mouth meat with gravy? OH-MY-GOODNESS-THIS-IS-MAKING-ME-HUNGRY! Anyway, this meal makes your house smell great and is the sort of meal your Mom probably made.

What you'll need:
4 large carrots
5 potatoes
1 onion
3 lb roast, (sirloin, rump, inside round)
Salt, pepper, garlic salt, oregano
1 cup water
1 cup beef broth or consommé
½ cup red wine

What you'll do:
1. Wash your hands.
2. Wash and peel the carrots
3. Wash and peel the potatoes
4. Peel and cut the onion into sections
5. Place the roast in a pan (you can do this on top of the stove in the roasting pan). Sear it on all sides.
6. When the all sides are brown, season it lightly with salt, pepper, garlic salt, and some oregano (never forget the oregano!).
7. Add about 1 cup of water, 1 cup of beef broth (consommé, if you have it) and a ½ cup of red wine into the roasting pan.
8. Put the covered roasting pan into a preheated oven at 350 F. Set the timer for an hour a pound. After two hours, check the roast's temp (you want 160F.).

9. Take the cover off at the halfway point of cooking, add the carrots, onions and potatoes by placing them around the edges of the roast. Add more liquid (a cup or so). Replace cover and put back in oven.

You shouldn't need a knife with this meal, except to butter some hot bread or crescent rolls.

You could put the vegetables in a bowl and put them, covered, into the oven while you're carving the roast, so they're still warm when you're ready to serve.

Tip

1   Periodically check the roast to ensure it's not running out of liquid. The important thing with a pot roast is you're after a certain texture – you want the beef to be able to fall off the roast.

This is one of those guaranteed-to-work meals that are designed for beginners. The fact it's tastier than hell makes it a happy and obvious entry in this section.

What you'll need:

3 lb bottom round beef roast
(if you're not sure when you buy it, mention to the butcher you're making a pot roast – he/she may advise you of a cut that's on sale)
2 large potatoes, peeled and cubed
2 large carrots, peeled and sliced
1 packet dry onion soup mix
½ cup water
¼ cup red wine
2 ½ feet aluminum foil

What you'll do:

1. Wash your hands.
2. Preheat oven to 300 degrees F (150 degrees C).
3. Into the bottom of a 9"x13" roasting pan, center the foil, shiny side up. Place the roast on the foil in the pan.
4. Place the cubed potatoes and carrots around the roast.
5. In a separate bowl, combine the onion soup mix with water. Mix well and pour over the roast.
6. Sprinkle roast with red wine.
7. Fold foil over and seal all edges.
8. Put uncovered into oven.
9. Bake for 4 hours.

Be sure to have some fresh bread on hand for this meal.

A Saturday Night Beef
["Honey, if I make dinner,
will you stop yelling at me?"]

Or, on second thought, perhaps it would be safer to say, "Hey, have a seat, I'll make dinner."

What you'll need:
½ cup butter or non-hydrogenated margarine
2 tablespoons garlic, minced
2 onions, sliced
1 green pepper, chopped
4 lbs lean steak, cut into 1" cubes
1 medium-size (14 ½ oz) can crushed or diced tomatoes

What you'll do:
1. Wash your hands.
2. Preheat oven to 325 degrees F (165 degrees C).
3. In a large skillet over medium heat, melt butter or margarine.
4. Add garlic, onion and green pepper and sauté for about 5 minutes.
5. Add meat and brown.
6. Transfer mixture to a medium-size casserole dish.
7. Pour the tomatoes over the mixture.
8. Cover, place in oven and bake for about 2 hours.

Slap this on top of white rice or egg noodles.

Homemade
Shepherd's Pie

Although we can easily buy this product in the frozen food section, there are times you have to test yourself. There are times you just have to. Why? Because it's there, dammit. Shepherd's Pie is also one of those meals my Mom made all the time that everyone loved. This is a real tasty meal and is easy to make – and it's healthier than the chemical-filled frozen ones. If you have one of those large, deep skillets that has a removable handle and a glass lid (which, in case you're wondering, I do!), use it here, especially if you don't have a crowd to feed.

What you'll need:
6 large potatoes
small splotch olive oil (when browning regular ground beef in a
 nonstick pan, oil is not really necessary because the meat's
 fat releases quickly. I like to add a little olive oil when
 browning lean ground beef because of taste and because
 there isn't as much fat in the meat)
2 lbs lean ground beef (or the pot roast leftovers)
1 cup frozen corn
2 tablespoons of butter or non-hydrogenated margarine
1 teaspoon oregano
salt and pepper to taste

What you'll do:
1. Wash your hands.
2. Wash and peel the potatoes.
3. Put them in a pot of water and boil for about ½ an hour.
4. Preheat oven to 325 degrees F.
5. In a large skillet over medium heat, cook ground beef (or heat up the pot roast leftovers that you have shredded into manageable pieces – here's a job for your manual food processor)
6. Drain off the excess oil and mix in the frozen corn. Stir well.
7. Transfer the mixture into an oven-ready casserole dish.
8. Once the potatoes are done, mash them with butter, and place on top of the meat/corn. Spread potatoes evenly.
9. Sprinkle with oregano, salt and pepper.
10. Put into oven for about an hour.

So, if we add these times up, we're about the same as a frozen shepherd's pie, which takes about 65–70 minutes. The only real difference is the time you'd have to spend preparing the handmade version, about 30 minutes or so if you're quick, versus, oh, 30 seconds it takes to rip open a package and put it into the oven, but at least you won't be consuming monogliceride decompresivoidinal – or some other completely unrecognizable additive.

Tip

1   You can speed up the cooking time for boiling potatoes by cutting them into quarters.

This dish reminds me of my ski club days while in my teens, when a couple of the socially advanced members actually made lasagnas every time we had a party! Having peers who could feed themselves and the occasional passer-by was very impressive, so I'm hoping you get a lot of mileage out of this embarrassingly easy-to-make recipe. As a footnote, you'd have a tough time finding someone who was a capable cook in their teens who didn't make something of themselves later on in life: one of them is now a high profile lobbyist and the other is a well-known fashion designer (it's up to you to determine gender, but I bet your guess would be wrong).

This recipe has to be good to compare to the frozen lasagnas available now, but remember, this one's homemade and unless you include a number of unpronounceable chemical additives, it'll be healthier.

What you'll need:
1 small (as opposed to the family pak) container of cottage cheese
1 small container ricotta cheese
1 egg
1 tablespoon garlic powder
1 tablespoon basil
2 tablespoons oregano
2 tablespoons olive oil
1 clove fresh garlic, minced
1 small onion, peeled and chopped
1 ½ lbs lean ground beef
1 jar of spaghetti sauce
1 package precooked oven-ready lasagna noodles
¾ of a 1 pound package grated mozzarella cheese

What you'll do:
In essence, you're assembling something from 3 different sources: the cheese stuff from a mixing bowl, the ground beef and spaghetti sauce from the skillet, and the pasta from the package.

You need: 1 large casserole dish (9"x12")
             1 large skillet
             1 mixing bowl

1. Wash your hands.
2. In mixing bowl, add cottage and ricotta cheese, egg (break on edge of bowl, open and allow contents to fall into bowl, then chuck shells). Mix well. Add garlic powder, basil and oregano. Mix well. Now you have your bowl of cheesy stuff.
3. In a large skillet over medium heat, bring oil up to temperature. Add garlic and onion, brown for one minute. Add ground beef and cook thoroughly. Drain off excess fat from ground beef. Add spaghetti sauce. Stir well. Now you have your meat source.
4. In the rectangle casserole dish, put a layer of the ground beef sauce.
5. Then put a layer of the noodles.
6. Then a layer of the cheese mixture.
7. Repeat steps 3 to 5.
8. End up with a layer of sauce, over which you will sprinkle the grated mozzarella cheese.

Beef Stroganoff

The first time I had this dish was at the Troika Restaurant in Montreal, which, if you've never been there, is a fantastic place to go. This was back in the early days of Glasnost, so one couldn't help but feel the owners – who were all Soviet Union ex-pats – were questioning their decision to open a restaurant that catered to culturally deficient English-speaking weenies. At any rate, whoever you make this meal for will appreciate the heritage of it, and if they don't seem too impressed, suggest they make a McCain's frozen pizza instead.

What you'll need:
2 tablespoons flour
1 teaspoon paprika
½ lb lean round steak
1 tablespoon olive oil
½ cup chopped onion
1 teaspoon crushed garlic
½ cup sliced mushrooms (use a tin to speed things up if you want)
1 cup sour cream
1 beef bouillon cube

What you'll do:
1. Wash your hands.
2. Mix flour and paprika in a closeable sandwich bag – or a Lock and Lock container.
3. Slice beef in thin diagonal strips.
4. Add beef strips to flour mixture and shake to coat.
5. Heat oil in a skillet over medium heat.
6. Once up to heat, add to skillet coated beef strips, onion and garlic, and brown.
7. Once meat is browned, stir in mushrooms, sour cream and crumbled bouillon cube. Heat to a boil, stirring constantly.
8. Reduce heat and simmer for 10 to 15 minutes until sauce is reduced and thickened.

It is an indisputable law that you must have egg noodles with this, by the way.

Veal Marsala

This is a meal that almost everyone who has been to an Italian restaurant has heard of, if not ordered at some time. When you mention to your date, wife, friend or self that you're making this meal, you'll instantly create a sense of appreciation that you're doing something a little bit special for them. It doesn't matter that this recipe is embarrassingly easy to make.

What you'll need:
½ cup all-purpose flour
a couple shakes of salt and pepper
½ lb veal scallops/scaloppini, about 1/8" thick
1 tablespoon olive oil
1 cup Marsala wine (or Sherry if you're at your grandmother's house)
1 cup chicken or vegetable broth

What you'll do:
1. Wash your hands.
2. Measure the flour in a measuring cup.
3. Add the salt and pepper. Stir it around to mix.
4. Pour the seasoned flour onto a dinner plate and spread around.
5. Lie the veal flat on the flour to coat it, turn over and coat the other side.
6. Shake off excess flour.
7. Heat oil in skillet.
8. Add veal and sauté about a minute on each side.
9. Once cooked, remove to a platter and cover to keep warm.
10. Add Marsala wine to veal pan. Let boil for a few minutes to thicken.
11. Add the cup of chicken or vegetable stock, and boil for a few more minutes.

Snow peas, green beans or asparagus go well with this meal, as opposed to, say, carrots and broccoli (try to use vegetables you don't have very often).

Don't forget to steam the green beans or asparagus rather than using the microwave (remember that business about nutrient loss in microwave ovens compared to steaming). Also, don't forget it's best to undercook vegetables because nothing's quite as gross as overcooked vegetables – especially asparagus.

It's not often you get a chance to use the word Conqueror in a sentence, so that's why I thought it would be fun here. You'll be a conqueror, too, when you sit down to eat this, because I'm pretty sure you'll conquer the entire thing in one sitting.

What you'll need:
2 mild Italian (or hot, if you're a maniac) sausages
1 ½ tablespoons olive oil
4 potatoes, peeled and cubed
2 carrots, chopped
1 onion, chopped
3 15 oz cans crushed or diced tomatoes
1 ½ teaspoons salt
¼ teaspoon ground black pepper
¼ teaspoon dried oregano

What you'll do:
1. Wash your hands.
2. Preheat oven to 375 degrees F (190 degrees C).
3. Remove casings from sausages and cut into 1" pieces.
4. In a large skillet over medium heat, add oil and bring up to temperature.
5. Add sausages when oil is hot. Sauté until nice and brown.
6. Place these into a 9"x12" casserole dish.
7. Layer the combination of potatoes, carrots and onions over the sausages. Then pour the can of tomatoes (and its juice) over all. Season with salt, ground black pepper and oregano.
8. Cover and bake for 60 minutes.
9. Uncover and bake for 20 more minutes.

Pasta Putanesca

Here is an incredibly fast, incredibly cheap meal that tastes gourmet. My nephew tells me this pasta was reputedly a favorite of Italian "ladies of the night." It may be best not to share this with your wife/date/etc. as you're serving it for dinner – unless your wallet's safely put away.

What you'll need:
olive oil
1 medium onion
2 cloves garlic
1 can diced tomatoes
your favorite herbs to season (see below)
freshly ground black pepper
¼ cup red wine (optional)
1 or 2 medium (or hot, if you're a maniac) Italian sausages
black olives – Kalamata are good (check the deli section,
    anything but canned will do)
capers
salt and pepper to taste
your favorite pasta (rotini works well)

What you'll do:
1. Wash your hands.
2. Remove sausage from casing and break into small pieces (it will look almost like ground beef when you're done). You can use a knife to slice the sausage the length of it and peel.
3 Sauté the onion and garlic in olive oil over medium heat until translucent (clear).
4. In a separate medium sized frypan over medium heat, add olive oil, and when up to heat, brown sausages.
5. Add diced tomatoes (for a thicker sauce, drain most of the juice from the can before adding tomatoes).
6. Add your favorite herbs (rosemary, basil, oregano, thyme, etc.) and freshly ground black pepper.
7. If you are having red wine with your meal, add a splash to the sauce.
8. Reduce heat and simmer until sauce begins to thicken.

9. Add sausage and olives (and capers if using).
10. Try not to stir too much or the tuna and olives will disintegrate.
11. Serve over top of your favorite cooked pasta.

Note: You don't have to peel the sausage if you don't want to; you could just slice it the way you would a carrot, but they will fall apart while browning anyway.

Risotto

This traditional Italian dish has a high UWR (Upfront Work Required) rating, but well worth the effort. Although it is just fancied-up rice, dates seem to find it irresistible. You can serve this as a main dish, or as a side.

What you'll need:
1 tablespoon olive oil
2 cloves garlic, finely chopped
1 small onion, finely chopped
1 cup short-grain rice (look for Arborio – it costs a little more
    but is essential for its creamy texture)
2–3 cups chicken stock
dash of salt, lots of fresh ground pepper
½ cup Parmesan cheese

What you'll do:
1. Wash your hands.
2. Sauté onion and garlic in olive oil over medium heat until translucent.
3. Add the rice and stir until coated with the onion mixture.
4. Add enough chicken stock to barely cover the rice, reduce the heat to medium-low and cover.
5. Stir often, and continue adding stock, a bit at a time, to keep the rice very moist, almost soupy, but not swimming.
6. Add fresh ground pepper and salt to taste.
7. Cook until rice is firm, but not crunchy (the Italians call it *al dente*), and is a nice, creamy texture.
8. Add Parmesan, and stir until combined.
9. Serve with good Italian bread and a nice red wine. You can use it as a side dish or with a salad, as a main.

Tip

1. There are as many varieties of risotto as there are pizzas. Experiment to find what ingredients you like best. For example, mushrooms are simple and elegant; adding cooked seafood (mussels, clams and shrimp for example) is decadent.

2. If using mushrooms, seafood, etc., add in the last few minutes so as not to overcook.

3. Fresh or dried herbs like rosemary, basil, and/or oregano, are a nice touch.

Ratatouille

This is kind of midway between a vegetarian meal and an elaborate vegetable dish. It's so good, you'll love it no matter what category you put it in.

What you'll need:
3 tablespoons olive oil
1 onion, chopped
1 clove garlic, minced
1 eggplant, diced
1 zucchini, cut in quarter rounds
1 pepper, diced
1 teaspoon dried basil
1 teaspoon dried oregano
¼ teaspoon dried thyme
1 can tomatoes
salt & pepper

What you'll do:
1. Wash your hands.
2. Wash and cut all vegetables.
3. In a large, deep skillet, bring oil up to temperature over medium heat.
4. Add and sauté onions until transparent.
5. Add garlic, and eggplant. Cook about 5 minutes, stirring often.
6. Add a little water (a couple of tablespoons) to the bottom of the pot to prevent sticking. Continue to cook until eggplant is fully cooked.
7. Add zucchini, peppers, and herbs.
8. When all vegetables are tender, add tomatoes.
9. Let vegetables stew another 15–20 minutes. Add more liquid, if necessary – water, stock, tomato juice, your choice.
10. Add salt and pepper to taste.

Sides & Sauces

Choosing which protein to have with dinner is pretty easy, as is choosing the vegetable. The challenge and the reward lie in the choice and execution of a side dish and the occasional sauce. We put so much focus on being able to make a tasty, well-cooked piece of chicken or meat, some lovely asparagus and ... what? Not every meal will have a sauce, of course, but being able to assemble one makes you Mom-like indeed. Side dishes and sauces are two things that can single-handedly elevate a decent meal into a "damn this is good!" meal. Being able to consistently choose a side dish that doesn't require the computing power of Big Blue to figure out and an enormous amount of preparation time is a sought-after skill. There are some prepared side dishes out there that are great – the Lipton SideKicks Scalloped Potatoes and Uncle Ben's Fast and Fancy Flavored Rices are sure bets.

My aim with this chapter is to provide a couple of suggestions on how to improve each of the side dish staples, and give you an idea of how to easily create some simple sauces.

Sides

Let's think for a moment about what kinds of side dishes we like, that some of us grew up with, regardless of whether there's a packaged version of it. In essence, there are four staples side dishes are made of:

> Pasta
> Rice
> Potatoes
> Beans

At the beginner level, of course, everything's an accomplishment: making pasta that's properly cooked, being able to time your rice so it isn't like cream of wheat cereal or a block of concrete, and making potatoes that don't bend forks as you try to pierce them – everything deserves praise and a pat on the back. The reason there are so many choices of packaged side dishes is because we're all subject to the law of diminishing returns: have something – even something you love – too often and one day you'll wake up craving a change. So, I'm going to show you how to take one step up with each of the basic sides.

We've all seen the packaged side dishes, like the SideKicks, Rice-a-Roni and Fast and Fancy Rices. Because I know you care deeply about my personal preferences, here are the ones that my boys and I could each eat an entire package of at a sitting:

SideKicks: Scalloped Potatoes
Fast and Fancy   Broccoli and Cheese Rice

I don't like any of the pasta ones because either I can never get the timing right so the pasta turns out weird, or the pasta is just plain weird regardless of the timing; also, I like to be able to dictate the pasta-to-sauce ratio, something you can't get from a package. Grocery stores will vary on which prepared side dishes they carry, so instead of giving you a detailed list, just go to the side dish section in your grocery store to find the ones they carry.

Pasta

Here are some ideas to make even simple pasta do something different:

- If all you do is boil the water, put the pasta in, wait for it to cook, drain it, put into bowls and top with your sauce, then try something different: once the pasta is cooked and drained, put it back into the pot and put either all or some of the sauce in and stir it around. I know this is basic, but if you haven't done it, it's a great change.
- If you always only make pasta and a heavy sauce, try cooking and draining the pasta and then adding either a bit of butter or olive oil and some shakable cheese (Parmesan or Romano) along with some herbs, stir it up and voila!, something different.
- If you always use the same pasta, use something different, like angel hair pasta, something few people use.

Rice

As a complement to a meal that has texture and sauces or liquids, rice is an unbeatable side dish. Usually if people want a change with rice, they buy the flavored stuff, which is great if the protein and vegetables are pretty uncomplex in their flavors, but is there anything you can do to help simple white rice take a minor step up?

- Add vegetable or chicken stock to the water.
- Sauté some vegetables (say, broccoli flowers and something else small) in olive oil and then toss into your cooked rice and keep tossing (until it's thoroughly mixed).

Potatoes

I've always liked potatoes because they're so comforting. Here are some obvious and not-so-obvious ways of preparing potatoes:

- Boiled
- Baked (either in foil or naked)
- Scalloped
- Fried
- Mashed
- Microwaved
- Placed in olive oil in a glass casserole dish, sprinkled with garlic salt and herbs and roasted in the oven (using the small red potatoes). Here's the recipe:

Awesome Potatoes

What you'll need:
10 or so small red potatoes (good for two people or
    just me if I'm hungry)
½ cup of olive oil
sprinkle of rosemary or oregano
sprinkle of garlic powder/garlic salt

What you'll do:
1. Wash the potatoes.
2. Place them in a casserole dish.
3. Add the olive oil. Roll the potatoes around to coat in oil.
4. Sprinkle on the rosemary or oregano and garlic powder.
5. Make sure there's about 1/8 of an inch of oil in bottom of dish.
6. Place in a preheated oven (350F) for ½ an hour, testing to make sure a fork can easily pierce them.

Beans

I'll admit I'm not a big bean person – my upbringing was pretty much rice and potatoes and much quieter than when I have beans, so you won't find personal testimonials here. I've asked a few friends of my girlfriend for some good recipes that involve beans, and here they are. These are great alternatives if you've spent a great deal of your time making pasta, potatoes or rice and you feel it might be time for a change. In no special order:

Texas Style BBQ Baked Beans

Here's a perfect meal to make after a day outside as a stand-alone meal with crusty bread and a salad, or as a side dish to roast beef and vegetables.

What you'll need:
2 large (19 oz) cans baked beans
½ cup smoke flavored BBQ sauce
½ cup brown sugar (now the kids are interested!)
1 generous shake of Worcestershire sauce

What you'll do:
1. Put the beans in a medium or large saucepan.
2. Heat until bubbling.
3. Add all other ingredients. Stir well.
4. Cook for 10 minutes.

Almost a Meal Beans

This recipe is good if you're in the mood for vegetarian fare, because it could be a meal unto itself, but it's also awesome with fish.

What you'll need:
small splash of olive oil
cup of chopped onion
1 green pepper, minced
2 cloves of garlic, minced
½ teaspoon salt
5 tablespoons tomato paste

Almost a Meal Beans (continued)

15 oz can of kidney beans (read the directions below
    before draining!)
1 cup uncooked white rice

What you'll do:
1. Wash your hands.
2. In a large saucepan over medium heat, heat oil.
3. Sauté onion, pepper and garlic until onion is translucent.
4. Add salt and tomato paste.
5. Reduce heat to low and cook 2 minutes.
6. Drain the beans, putting the liquid aside. Stir in beans and rice.
7. Pour the liquid into a measuring cup and add water to reach a
    volume of 2 ½ cups.
8. Pour this liquid into beans. Cover.
9. Cook on low for 45 minutes.
1-. The liquid should be absorbed and the beans and rice should
    be cooked.

Triple Bean Casserole

What you'll need:

½ lb bacon
1 lb lean ground beef
1 onion, chopped
¾ cup brown sugar
½ cup ketchup
1 teaspoon dry mustard
1 tablespoon vinegar (white)
15 oz can baked beans
15 oz can kidney beans
15 oz can lima (butter) beans

What you'll do:
1. Wash your hands.
2. In a large, deep skillet, cook bacon over medium-high heat
    until thoroughly brown.
3. Drain, dry and break into 1"–2" pieces, then set aside.
4. Brown ground beef.

5. Combine browned ground beef and bacon pieces. Stir until mixed.
6. Preheat the oven to 350F.
7. Put the beef/bacon mixture into a large bowl and stir in the sugar, ketchup, vinegar, mustard, and the 3 cans of beans with their respective liquids. Mix thoroughly.
8. Transfer mixture into large casserole dish (9"x13").
9. Bake uncovered for 1 hour.

Sauces

I have a confession to make: this section only came about because I recently made a sauce to go along with my wok dinner and IT WAS AMAZING. Without any exaggeration, it was the best thing I'd ever prepared, and my girlfriend, who's competitively blasé about my cooking, raved as well. In the past, the history of sauces has interfered with my ability to enjoy them (sauces were originally created to cover up the gamey meat cooks had to work with before refrigeration, so I tended to view them as a cover-up for inferior meat). Even without my preoccupation with history, I've regarded sauces as something other people do and an unnecessary extravagance. But, while we're likely never going to be confused with Cordon Bleu cooks, we can still nod briefly in their direction, as in, knowing how to make a sauce.

The first challenge for beginner cooks is to know which sauces go with what meals – doesn't matter how the sauces came about. The next challenge is how to make your own sauces without having to spend too much time doing them. We want the quiet sleeper sauce we can do while talking to whoever's in the kitchen, the ones we can make without any apparent effort. Sauces are something that both Moms and experienced, well-trained cooks can do in a heartbeat, and, just as Lipton's SideKicks dominate the side dish aisle, you can find walls of prepackaged sauces that only require the addition of water.

But I'm talking about a midway point between the sauces our Moms made from scratch and the convenience of ripping open a package, pouring the contents into a saucepan and adding water. To my way of thinking, there are a few things you should know, should you decide to spruce things up with sauces. There are 5 basic sauces from which many other variations can stem, 5 sauces that my niece, Lori (who graduated from George Brown School of Culinary Arts in Toronto), describes as being "as old as rocks." This sauce section is a little more sophisticated because it's Lori's specialty. Here are the 5 essential sauces (they're described below):

Espagnole	brown sauce
Velouté	a light stock base
Béchamel	basic white sauce
Hollandaise	one step up from basic
Tomato	no comment required (so many to choose from)
Gravy	I'm adding gravy as the sixth, in case you haven't made it yet

I think it's important to give a little background here, because this sauce business is a little more complex than I first imagined. The key terms for sauces are:

Deglaze	Let's say you've sautéed a chicken breast and you've removed the chicken from the pan. On the bottom are food particles from the cooking process. Now, if you add a little wine and stock to the pan and use a wooden spoon to unstick the food particles from your pan, you are now **deglazing**. Bear in mind, don't use high heat if you've included wine, unless you're planning to see what you look like without eyebrows (it may catch fire). This is what the pros do to achieve great tastes, mainly because of the flexibility inherent in the process: you can use almost any liquid – wine, alcohol, stock, juice, etc. – and whatever else you want to chuck in there for taste, along with a thickener and spices and off you go.
Glaze	This is when you take some sort of sweet jam/jelly/marmalade/red pepper jelly/your Aunt Edna's juicy strawberry jam and drop a dab on a chop, or about a ¼ cup on tenderloin halfway through the cooking time. The sugars caramelize and it's damn tasty.
Reduce	You'll remember this term from the cooking terms section. All you're doing is low boiling the liquid to reduce the quantity and increase the taste. Here you could add some butter to thicken and improve the taste. Honestly, you have to do this for yourself

before you realize how easy it is and how unfathomably tasty it is.

Pan sauce	This is what you end up with when you've done the deglaze/reduce steps, something with which you should become very familiar because it's easy and it's great. This is where you can be as inventive as you want. When you're making your own pan sauce for some pork chops, try some white wine, stock and some tangerines, or cranberries.
Thickeners	cornstarch and water = slurry equal parts butter and flour = roux

Sauce	Description
Espagnole	This is what you're talking about when you refer to "brown sauce." This is the sauce you'll start with as a base before you add peppercorns and cream to make a peppercorn sauce, or mushrooms and sour cream for beef stroganoff. Because they demand an enormous commitment of time to make from scratch, our sauce lady says packaged ones are fine, with *The Green Peppercorn* from Knorr and *Demi Glace* from Stouffer being the top picks. Lori's trick: add ¼ cup of cup of red wine, along with the cream or sour cream, or whatever they recommend on the package.
Velouté	This refers to a light stock base. Even at my crop-duster level of cooking, I've found stocks to be my best flavor-enhancing trick.
Béchamel	is your basic white sauce. You can add cheese to the sauce as a base for homemade mac & cheese, and you can use it for chicken à la king. This is, according to Lori, very easy to make on your own: 2 tablespoons butter 2 tablespoons flour 1 cup milk salt to taste

• Melt butter on low heat, add flour slowly, mixing well; cook on low heat. Add warmed milk slowly.

Hollandaise   You can easily find a packaged version of this, but apparently they aren't as good as what you could whack together in your blender. This sauce is great on fish/steak/asparagus. Here's Lori's blender version:
1 cup butter
4 egg yolks
¼ teaspoon each of salt, sugar, tabasco and dry mustard
2 tablespoons fresh lemon juice

• Heat butter to boil, but don't brown.
• Combine all other ingredients.
• With blender running, slowly pour butter into yolk mixture in a thin stream until all is added and let it chat for a while in the blender.

Tomato   You've got many choices here – prepared sauces, make your own – so I'd rather discuss something you may not know.

Gravy   This approach to gravy making works for any meat or poultry. So, you'll be able to roast a chicken, roast beef, have a turkey dinner and make a great gravy. Here's what Lori does:

Take the roast or whatever out of its roasting pan. While it is "standing" (juices settling), put the roasting pan on a stove element and turn to medium high. Deglaze with 1–2 cups of liquid (as my family creates a veritable stew-on-a-plate with Sunday dinner, I make a lot of gravy). With the liquid and all simmering, sprinkle in the Veloutine [you can use flour if you don't have any relative of the Velour family in your kitchen cupboard]. Magically, after a few minutes of stirring, it will be thick and tasty. Some more refined people may strain theirs before serving, but why – the lumps are tasty.

But what are some ideal match-ups?

Meat	Sauce
Red meat	Peppercorn sauce
	Demi-glace
Grilled chicken	Lemon cream sauce
	White wine and stock deglaze
Pork chops/roast	Fruit-flavored glaze, with tarragon
Fish	Hollandaise

This information is merely meant to get you started on the path to becoming a sauce-maker; my intention is not to give you endless match-ups, but to give you a leg up on the whole business of sauces. Now it's up to you to give them a go!

Stuff To Clean It Up With: Get It Back in the Bag

I'd be a bald-faced liar if I told you I love cleaning. I do, however, enjoy walking into the house when it's tidy and clean and nice smelling. So, the $64,000 question, the challenge to beat all challenges, the for-my-next-magical-trick-I-will-become-someone-I'm-not, is how can I get the best possible job done if I'm not really fond of doing it? I feel the answer can only be found in approaching the task as a military commander would: find the technology that'll do the work for us. There are no awards for hand-to-hand cleaning combat, the way there are for homemade piecrusts at county fairs. There's no victory lap at the end of spending an entire day doing everything by hand. No, there's just whatever time we spend cleaning that could be spent doing something we enjoy.

So, we're after the easiest and the best: the easiest way to get a job done, the fastest and the best way of doing it. We're after the cleaning tools that make us, the real life Tim or Tina the Tool Man, happy. If we could turbo-boost the vacuum and have it operate by robot or virtually from our work computer, great. If there were a way of cleaning the bathroom floor by opening the door a crack, throwing in a cleansing cluster bomb and slamming the door shut, we'd buy it. Or if they could invent a "smart cleaner," along the lines of "smart bombs" (that knew where the evil germs were hiding without us having to provide the ground support), that would be our way of cleaning.

While some of that is fantasy, in fact, the products on the market now give us cleaning non-keeners such an advantage it's almost unfair. Note, I said almost. So, let's go through the cleaning products and their uses and then I'll show you a schedule you could consider for deploying your new arsenal.

To instill a sense of purpose, along with your sense of humor, focus on the three areas of concern:

- Bacteria
- Allergies
- Grossness

So, let's call it the BAG3 (BAG to the 3rd Power – hey if it can't be fun, at least have fun talking about it) rule of cleaning. Simply, if we deal with the harmful bacteria in the house – usually the kitchen – if we address the dust that can cause or exacerbate allergies, and we eliminate things we don't want to step in, we're done, baby!

For the Bacteria

Kitchen: Top on anyone's list these days should be food safety and ensuring the bacteria that follows your groceries into the house is ushered back out of the house. You'd have to be an enormous (dangerous) optimist to believe most meats, poultry and vegetables have NOT come into contact with harmful bacteria somewhere along their very long line of processing to packing to storage to packing again to the store to your home. Normal cooking is going to kill the bacteria, don't worry; what I'm concerned about is ensuring work areas and kitchen counters are sanitary. The biggest mistake people make is with their dishcloth. They leave it on their faucet for weeks on end, using it to clean up spilt raw chicken or raw ground beef, then give their cloth a little rinse, clean their fingers with the cloth and put a carrot stick into their mouth – using the same fingers, of course, that have just held a cloth that has raw meat remnants on it. Or, they use their dishcloth to wipe raw meats off the cutting board, give it a little rinse, wipe off the counter and then put food they're preparing on the counter that again has raw meat remnants.

Bacteria Most of what the average person knows about household cleaners and bacteria is based on what their mother told them or what they see on TV. The claims made by brands we've grown up with are the claims we live by. Indeed, if a brand says it eliminates 99.9% of household germs, we think that's good. Let's face it, if we graduated from high school math, we know that 99.9 is very close to 100, a perfect score. I've spent a fair amount of my time advising people to use cleaning products that make their lives easier and get the job done – i.e., make the place clean and eliminate harmful bacteria.

Unfortunately, I'm also influenced by what I see on TV, and it turns out the ads we see on TV or in the paper offer, at best, partial truths and at worst, apparent attempts to mislead. So, I spoke with Randy Pilon, CEO of Virox Technologies, the company that hospitals, cruise ships, dental offices and other such institutions call when they need a product that is 100% effective in eliminating bacteria – not the infamous 99.9%. Virox is well known as a provider of hospital-grade disinfectants. Here's my take on a few things Randy shared with me about household cleaners. There are four aspects of household cleaners and bacteria we should consider.

- The role of fragrance
- The notion of 99.9% effective
- The importance of label reading versus TV commercials
- Residual claims:
  - The story behind resistant organisms
  - "Sell points"
  - How we're contributing to stronger bugs

Fragrance ... Randy mentioned that in focus groups, if a group was given two products to use as a cleaner, one, a bottle containing distilled water with a nice fragrance, and the other, an effective cleaner with little or no scent, they would say the first product cleaned best. Fragrance has become such an enormous business that it is now the determining factor behind "successful" cleaners, regardless of whether they work or not. So, smell clean = is clean for the majority of consumers.

The notion of 99.9% as a winning number. High school math will tell us that 99.9% is a damn good score, with that remaining 0.1% being withheld by a cranky teacher. In fact, 99.9 in the microbial world is a dismal failure; 99.9 in the scientific world is a miss, not a hit. Hospitals don't accept 99.9%. Dental offices don't say, "Wow, your product is close enough, I'll order a case." They accept 99.9999%, but not 99.9%. Why is this relevant? Advertising, my dear Watson. We want to believe in the numbers we see on TV. Imagine if a commercial reported that "4 out of 5 doctors recommend this product. We would have had 5 out of 5, but, unfortunately, the 5th doctor died."

Label reading versus TV commercials ... Ask anyone about antibacterial sprays or kitchen wipes and they'll say, "The commercial shows the person spraying and immediately wiping off the counter, or using the wipes, and that's what I do." Well, take a look at the label. The label says the sprayed or wiped area has to stay wet for 10 minutes in order to be effective as an antibacterial product. Ten minutes. What's one of the ingredients? Alcohol. Try keeping an area wet with a product that has alcohol in it. The point is, the commercials would have you believe all you have to do is spray and wipe, and maybe wait 30 seconds. But on the label, in very small print, it will tell you that if the area doesn't remain wet for 10 minutes, the product acts only as a cleaner, which is fine, except it's being touted as an antibacterial.

Residual claims ... The story behind resistant organisms, "sell points" and how we're contributing to stronger bugs. Nobody likes the fact that antibiotics aren't working as well as they once did. Nobody likes the fact that pesticides can't fight certain bugs anymore. Why is this happening? Because we pour millions of gallons of antibacterial cleaners down the drain every single day. We push the feeble bacteria to the outskirts and allow the strong bacteria to weight-lift their way closer and closer to the drain. We can do our part by refusing antibiotics for a cold or a viral bacteria because they have no effect on these things anyway. We can do our part by choosing soap for our hands and detergent for our dishes – minus the antibacterial agent. We can also avoid residual claims products that offer to "eliminate bacteria for 14 days." Do the bacteria tell each other to take a vacation until the 14 days are over? No. They're like Vikings; they get pushed further and further back until the opposition weakens, then they retaliate, gaining strength as they push back. Hospitals don't use "residual claims" products. They want the product to work now, eliminate bacteria, and then stop working within a minute. So, why are we as consumers being offered products that experts wouldn't use? Because the industry is driven by the "smells clean = is clean" consumer.

Is there a product that is 100% effective, one that stops working a minute after use, and one that doesn't give a false sense of security? My vote would go with a product that uses the same technology health institutions insist on – Virox Technologies' Accelerated Hydrogen Peroxide. The only consumer products using this technology are certain Orange Glo anti-bacterial products – look for the Accelerated Hydrogen Peroxide logo on the label. They may even have the product available in wipes.

Bathroom: These same trusty antibacterial wipes can be used with great success in the bathroom – on the sink, faucets, toilet base and so on (just be sure to be wearing rubber gloves, for no reason other than you too have sons around the house whose aim isn't what it should be).

In the bathroom you've got double duty: there's the Bacteria and there's also Grossness – especially if you have boys in the house. The absolute best way to clean a bathroom floor is with a **Swiffer Wetjet**. If there was one product that revolutionized house cleaning and allowed the domestically challenged to take a giant step up the ladder of home care, it would be the Swiffer Wetjet. For those of you who may have been shipwrecked for 5 years, the Wetjet is a floor-cleaning device that has a replaceable cleaning solution bottle that can be sprayed on the floor as you go, the spray being powered by batteries, along with a floor-cleaning pad that is replaceable when dirty. The beauty of the Wetjet is that you put the cleaning solution in, slap a cleaning pad on it and you can run through the house looking for offending floors. And I mean run: there's no danger of spilling the cleaning agent (within reason). Because there's very little room in my bathroom for negotiating around the toilet, I love the fact I can just wheel in there, squirt the juice, mop up and get out of Dodge – in less time than it would have taken me to walk gingerly up the stairs with a pail of hot water and cleaner.

Lysol has a **Poweron Gel** toilet bowl cleaner that I've found to work really well.

It's probably relevant to mention that **toilet-cleaning brushes** are products that don't exist in the eyes of most guys. The fact is that most guys (I doubt it's just me) have a tough time getting eye to eye with things they don't want to acknowledge exist. I could never figure out how toilets got clean until I lived with a woman (I'm kind of kidding). In fact, I even have one of those full face visors you can use when cutting trees and brush – just so nothing even remotely fecal flies in my face when cleaning the toilet. So, my recommendation on learning how to clean like a pro is to make sure you're totally protected from the nasties: gloves, brushes with super long handles, and cleaning products like the Poweron Gel that works as fast as you'd like it to, so you don't have to hunker down on all fours and have a meaningful chat with an open toilet.

For the Allergies

Dusting   If you or anyone you're responsible for has allergies, dusting is highly recommended. The irony with the dusting program, though, is that some people go so nuts with dusting spray, they've merely replaced one allergen with another, probably more harmful one. A terrific product to consider is the **Swiffer Duster**, for the following reasons:

- They capture dust, not move it from one place to another
- They don't require dusting spray
- They have an extendable handle to do places that usually require special tools
- They are so soft and pliable you can dust around delicate objects without having to secure them from getting broken.

I absolutely love these things because of how screamingly fast and efficient they are. Let's face it, it takes either a pretty determined dusting job to do the blades on a ceiling fan or the top slats of window blinds, or a specialized extendo-product that you only use once in while when you remember. Now you can use the extendable handle Swiffer Duster and look far more in control of things than you ever thought possible. Timesavings? Probably 65% over the conventional method of dusting.

For the Grossness

Floors   Dust bunnies and the like are, to my way of thinking, a depressant. Even more depressing is the thought I have to traipse downstairs and drag my 420-pound vacuum up the stairs for deployment. Instead, I'm pleased to report that technology has finally caught up with the Jetsons: I use the **Roomba** by iRobot, a robot vacuum that answers my very important need to get something done while not actually doing it. It is so much fun watching a piece of machinery do your work. It's got sensors that make it follow a wall, go around chair legs, and prevent it from wiping out down the stairs. It even has a virtual door for those doorways that are un-doored. This is a product that without a doubt answered many people's wish list. Watching a machine do your schlep-work is perversely satisfying. The Roomba works on a rechargeable battery and has a dirt chamber similar to a dust-buster that has to be emptied after every room.

If you don't have a Roomba or there is debris you don't want the Roomba to deal with, the original Swiffer offers the best solution. It's the one that has either a dry cloth thing or a wet cloth thing you secure to it and wipe the floor with. When you've accumulated as much kak as you can transport into one pick-up area, do the movie theatre thing with **Rubbermaid**'s **Long Handle Dustpan and Broom** – you know, the ones you see movie theatre attendants using to pick up offending particles on the floor they have no intention or interest in actually touching, that let you pick up a veritable pile of debris without even bending slightly? Those things are great. Especially if you like to preserve your knees for tennis, or some other sport that requires mobility.

And speaking of solutions, I forgot to mention that the Swiffer Wetjet has evolved: it now has a wood floor cleaning solution and a scrubbing head for those tough spots you've ignored a little longer than you should have. I never cease to be amazed at how quick the Swiffer Wetjet is and how much ground I can cover in such little time. I still think it's funny that I can do the entire kitchen floor and part of the hallway in less time than it would have taken me to find the bucket, the cleanser, fill the bucket with water, measure the cleanser and drag everything to the middle of the floor, only to trip over it as I back up.

One of the biggest criticisms of the Wetjet has been its inability to scrub things that have been left too long, something that has been addressed because the Wetjets now have a scrubbing pad that's kind of like one of those non-abrasive dish-scrubbing things. So, now you can invert the head and give a very strong scrub to something that escaped your attention for the week.

The other rooms I haven't covered are very straightforward: bedrooms, family rooms, etc. These are too easy to discuss. All you have to do is pick up the crap on the floors and let loose the Roomba. As that's happening, you can scour the room with your Swiffer Duster.

Best Cleaning Approach

Of course, even Pentagon-approved cleaning products will not win the war against dirt if you never go into battle with them. And it's not a reliable system to wait until things look dirty, even though I'm still of the wait-until-you-can-see-the-color-of-the-dirt-before-springing-into-action mindset, unfortunately.

So, for your cleaning enjoyment, consider the Life is a Schedule approach to cleaning. This approach will let you enjoy life while still staying a step ahead of the Health Board. And of course, for many of us, if it's not scheduled, it doesn't exist and therefore will not happen.

Simply, look at your schedule and break down the cleaning requirements. My goal with this schedule is give you a track to run on. Why? Sometimes it's easier to create and stick to a schedule rather than wait for inspiration – an especially perilous approach to things we don't like doing. Let's say these are the activities you have to do:

Dusting	How many rooms
Vacuuming	How many rooms
Bathrooms	How many
Kitchen	Floor, microwave, counters
Laundry	Lights, darks
Mirrors	How many
Floors	How many
Garbage	How many pails/what day is pick up. This garbage thing seems like a no-brainer: You just wait until the pails are full and take it out. The key deterrent to this approach is the lovely odor garbage develops, so this scheduled version precludes you having to be told to take out the stinky garbage.

Consider this schedule

Keep in mind, when I refer to washing bathroom floor on Monday at 6:30, I'm talking about a 2.5-minute exercise. When I refer to dusting with the Swiffer Duster, it's a 3-minute thing. So, this scheduling thing looks like a huge time undertaking, but it's not. Either way, I know this is asking a lot. It could be one of those things that on paper seem like a super idea. I'm not the best with schedules, so I feel a little hypocritical even suggesting one. But, in all fairness, this might be the best way of doing things.

	Monday	Tuesday	Wednesday	Thursday	Friday
6:00P	Dinner	Dinner	Dinner	Dinner	Dinner
6:30	Wash bath. Flr.		Soccer Practice		
7:00	Soccer Game	Run/gym	Laundry – lights		Run
8:00			Tennis Ladder		Tennis Ladder
9:00		Vacuum Bdrm	Wash kit. floor		
9:30	Mirrors			Bar Stool	Bar Stool
10:00	Clean kit. Sink	Clean kit. Sink	Clean kit. sink		

That's all I'm going to say on the schedule subject. It might serve some people really well. At any rate, regardless of WHEN you actually get around to cleaning, these are some products that will make your work a little easier.

A lot of people will notice the brand name products their Moms used and then in a fit of quasi-efficiency, will buy similar looking products at a dollar store. I'm not going to go into a long dissertation about my experiences with products that seem like a great deal, cost-wise, but end up doubling the time required and do half the job, so just take my word for it: brand name products do a better job.

Other products you'll find useful:

For the Dishes

Dishwasher ... Get one, even if you have to buy a secondhand one from a shop around the corner.

Scrubbing brush ... This going to make you so jealous: I have a **Dawn PowerBrush**, something that can best be described as a foot-long cordless screwdriver with a scrub brush – except this one's waterproof. You have to try this thing to believe it! Washing pots and stuff used to be a major pain in the behind, but not now. The fact you can wash something without getting your hands wet gets high marks.

Dish detergent ... Buy one that has a grease-cutting agent. Don't worry about getting one with an antibacterial agent. And buy the one that comes with a pump so you don't have to grab it with wet hands to squeeze some out.

Rubber gloves ... These are good if you're squeamish like me and don't like putting your hand into substances you're not sure of. The ones I bought aren't those girly ones that are yellow; I went to Home Depot and got some orange gloves that were really designed for working with toxic chemicals – they look tough.

Microwave oven ... **Easy Off** also has a good oven cleaner.

For the Laundry

Laundry basket ... From an ease-of-use standpoint, nothing can beat the **Rubbermaid Flex'n Carry Hamper**. If you've ever nearly lost your finger in the mesh of one of the old rectangle laundry baskets as you tried to pick it up when it was full, or it felt like you were wrestling an alligator on your hip, this product is great because you can carry it in one hand (unless, of course, your clothes are so highly stacked you're dusting the ceiling as you walk down the hall).

Detergent ... The best stuff I've ever used and the one most used by people who know laundry is **Tide**. This is the detergent your Mom, neighbor, girlfriend, wife, sister, mother-in-law, grandmother (do I have to go on?) uses. I think this is a good indicator of whether it works. It's a good product if you want to get your clothes clean without using a great deal of detergent and don't want allergic reactions. Bear two things in mind: less is best with detergent and wash underwear for at least 10 minutes – you can't get away with a Short Cycle for these things. Wanna know why? You sure? Fecal matter. It must be dealt with and it takes longer than a short cycle to vanquish the nasties. Lastly, don't forget to turn your black shirts or jeans inside out or they'll fade quickly and you'll be wearing the uniform of the Gray Flannelian rather than the Black Bohemian.

Fabric softener ... When we forge out into the world for ourselves, a lot of times we leave things that remind us of home. Things like self-cleaning bathrooms, magically appearing meals and nice smelling clothes. Fabric softener is a sure one-step fix to homesickness. Some people with allergies find those sheets a little rough, so get one of those Downy ball things that you can just chuck into your washing machine when you start it.

For the Ironing

Iron ... The iron I like best is the **T-Fal Ultraglide Iron**, which is better than my old cheap iron. I've noticed that – again – you get what you pay for, even in things as mundane as irons. The key thing is to have that Teflon or non-stick coating so it's fast and precise, which the Ultraglide is.

Ironing board ... Get a decent ironing board as well, and a better than average cover. Why? If it's too thin, you leave the design of the board on your shirts. They also last longer.

These products have all contributed to making my life as a reluctant domestic easier and more enjoyable. They will also let you operate at a much higher level of performance at a fraction of the time it takes to do identical tasks with "traditional" tools, something that gives me great pleasure. Cleaning still has to be done, for sure, but at least you know you're using the best technology has to offer and it's letting you be the best you can be, as utterly corny as that sounds.

I'd like to close my section on cleaning with this thought: generally speaking, any products developed by well-known companies will be good. For instance, Lysol now has a battery-powered toilet cleaning brush; Tide has a whirling brush/applicator, and so on. Both these products deserve a look and a try for one simple reason: they answer a need. Well-known companies have the manpower, talent and the resources to develop products that answer a real consumer need. They do focus testing to determine what part of your cleaning life can be improved and if enough of the focus groups say the same thing, they will bring out a product that answers that need. They're not always right, but they take your requirements seriously.

On the other hand, I'm going to caution you against buying imitations of a national brand. They're the products you see on late night TV and you know they're a rip-off of a trusted brand. They're like the generic pharmaceutical firms, where someone else had the vision and paid for the research to fill a real need, and these vultures just wait until they can rip the formula and make a cheaper one. If I sound opinionated, I am. I think it's cheap. I'd much rather pay for a brand that has made it their business to create and bring to market products people can have faith in, than rip something off.

So, for cleaning (and most things, for that matter), buy original, don't buy dollar store crap that looks similar to the national brands. Want another reason? If the thing breaks or doesn't do what it says it will do, wrap it up and send it back. You'll get your money back and an apology. Try that with "The Wet Bet Sniffer".

Last Words: Everything Needs Context

Now that you have an enlightened perspective on this domestic stuff, I'll bet two new words spring into mind: acknowledgement and appreciation. I think it takes knowing how to do something to be able to fully appreciate and acknowledge the efforts someone makes for you in these areas. I hope the information I've provided you with in this book allows you to become bolder and more creative in the kitchen; at least you now know the rules. And as an acting teacher of mine once said, "you have to know the rules before you can break them."

But with knowledge, there are challenges and responsibilities. The challenges come from managing your new abilities. I mean, if you're in a relationship where the other person's a great cook – doesn't matter if it's your wife, husband or roommate – how do you contribute? Will your contributions be accepted and appreciated, or will they constantly be offering suggestions and beating you to the pot (better than with it, I suppose)? When should you offer to make dinner? Conversely, what if you're the only person who can cook, and now you're doing a reverse June Cleaver thing? How can you encourage them to learn? Sometimes the person who's better at something gets the job, day after day, week after week, month after month – a surefire recipe for resentment. These things may sound trivial, but are the root of many relationships' troubles.

Why am I bringing this up? Because I live it firsthand: my girlfriend's a great cook and a lot of what I know is because of her, but now I can hold my own. Now I can make a great Valentines or special event dinner, along with the day-to-day meals. But how does that make her feel? How does that make any woman who's been brought up at the tail end of an era of defined gender roles – where women were in charge of the cooking? Is it a help or a challenge to her identity? Does it make her appreciative and acknowledge the contribution or is it a little confusing, unsettling, in a way no one could articulate? The same way it would be confusing for a guy whose wife or girlfriend is equally proficient with a power drill. Do we want to share our drills or is it annoying? Do we want to give praise for a task, or do we feel slighted because we weren't needed to do the job? I admit I certainly don't have the answer.

However, I do have a recommendation for people in a relationship or a home with other cooking-capable people: create a schedule – regardless of ability. You can save yourself, your roommates, your relationship, your family, your whatever, a huge amount of ultimate grief if you assign meal-making responsibilities. Help them, praise them, and acknowledge their efforts and it will go a long, long way to making their lives – and the lives of anyone they may live with, more harmonious.

Acknowledgements

Anytime someone appears to have an ounce of knowledge, it's probably wise to prepare for a detailed Acknowledgements page. I have to extend thanks to many people and institutions, and so, in no special order:

Lora Tamburri at Hushion House, who is always honest with what she thinks about my books and whose suggestions and contributions are always valuable. Bill Hushion at Hushion House, whose sense of humor is only surpassed by his knowledge of the book industry, and who started as a reluctant mentor and has become a friend. Karen Petherick of Intuitive Design, who somehow manages to make things look good. Penny Hozy, my editor, who has made this an easier read than it would have been without her. My niece, Lori Kennedy, provided substance to the Sauces section. My nephew, Michael Kennedy, who's input on the Label Reading and Fats sections, provided a terrific health perspective. Juanita Coumbias of Atlantic Promotions for having faith in me and my enthusiasm. Rami El Bayadi, Win Sakdinan and Joyce Law of Procter and Gamble, who illustrate that within huge companies, you can still find real, down-to-earth, people; I'm very proud of and grateful for their support. Mark Cator, a friend and CEO of Cardinal Meat Specialists, who's probably the only person I know more passionate than I am about food safety and certainly the only person who doesn't raise his eyes when I start talking about it.

The following websites have been terrifically resourceful and helpful:

www.fightbac.org	This site clearly expresses the importance and methods of proper food safety.
www.google.com	Clearly the best search engine.
www.dictionary.com	A great place to ensure you're using a wrong word on purpose.
www.fsis.usda.gov	US Department of Agriculture Food Safety and Inspection Service.
www.agctr.lsu.edu	LSU Agricultural Center's Nutrition Curriculum.

I hope I haven't missed anybody, and if I have, I owe you dinner!

Index

Recipes & Notes

Recipes & Notes

Recipes & Notes

Recipes & Notes

Recipes & Notes

Recipes & Notes

Recipes & Notes

Recipes & Notes

Home Ec for the Domestically Challenged